Thomas C. Higgins
A Man Reinvented
Farmer, Teacher, Artist
1902–1992

Tom, ca. 1925

Thomas C. Higgins
A Man Reinvented
Farmer, Teacher, Artist
1902–1992

Nancy Higgins Hall

Alive Book Publishing

Thomas C Higgins
A Man Reinvented
Copyright © 2025 by Nancy Higgins Hall

All rights reserved.
No part of this book may be reproduced or transmitted in any form or by any means without written permission from the publisher and editor.

Additional copies may be ordered from the publisher for educational, business, promotional or premium use. For information, contact ALIVE Book Publishing at: alivebookpublishing.com.

Book Design by Nancy Higgins Hall

ISBN 13
978-1-63132-272-3

First Edition

Published in the United States of America by
ALIVE Book Publishing
an imprint of Advanced Publishing LLC
3200 A Danville Blvd., Suite 204, Alamo, California 94507
alivebookpublishing.com

PRINTED IN THE UNITED STATES OF AMERICA

10 9 8 7 6 5 4 3 2 1

Contents

A Tribute (a poem by Rachel Higgins)..xiii
Preface...xv
Chapter 1: The Early Years..1
    Marriage Gone Awry...3
    Second Time Around...3
    Inescapable Schooling...5
    Tom's Grandpa..8
    Tom's First Ride from Horse to Horsepower..............................12
    Raising a Pig Can Change Your Life..13
Chapter 2: Traveling East..17
    Tom's Ticket to the Future..21
    Taking a Different Path: The Lure of the Farm..........................23
Chapter 3: A Blind Date..25
    An Adventurous Minister..25
    Fighting Debauchery...28
    On the Move Again...28
    Romance Blooms..29
    Childhood Traumas...29
    Off to College..32
    A Rocky Ride..34
    An Unexpected Friendship...36
    Graduation, But No Diploma..37
    Whoopee! Marriage...39
    Seeds of Hope, Fields of Disappointment..................................40
Chapter 4: Michigan to Maine..41
    The Schopflochers and the Bahá'í...44
    The Jealous Chauffeur...46

Chapter 5: On to Rhode Island..49
Chapter 6: East Farm...57
    The 1930s...57
    The Early 1940s...76
    World War II...85
    The Farm.. 95
    Usquepaug..100
Chapter 7: A Promise Kept..105
    Poultry Disease Research...113
    Dad's Interest in Paranormal Phenomena..124
    Back to Chickens..127
    Flying the Coop..127
    Exodus from the Farm..128
    A Blind Date and a Long Wait...133
    The Lure of the West..134
    Barbecue Expert..137
    Bosses Can Be a Pain...138
    Fraternity Woes..138
Chapter 8: New Endeavors..141
    The Travel Bug...144
    Returning to Art..145
    Growing Older..155
    Rachel's Pursuits...155
    Running Out of Steam..159
No Magic in Moondust (a poem by Rachel Higgins).............................219
Acknowledgments..221
Index..225

List of Photos

Cover Photo: Tom, ca. 1950
Photo 1: James T. Higgins, 1807–1898, Tom's Paternal
  Great-Grandfather xviii
Photo 2: Mary A. Higgins, 1813–1872, Tom's Paternal
  Great-Grandmother xviii
Photo 3: Lucius Rathbun, 1800–1875, Tom's Paternal
  Great-Grandfather xix
Photo 4: Sarah Glick, 1813–1891, Tom's Paternal
  Great-Grandmother xix
Photo 5: Thomas Titus Higgins, 1844–1916, Tom's Paternal
  Grandfather xx
Photo 6: Caroline Rathbun, 1846–1934, Tom's Paternal
  Grandmother... xx
Photo 7: Samuel Nathaniel Palmer, 1829–1898, Tom's Maternal
  Grandfather xxi
Photo 8: Margaret E. Wiley, 1841–1914, Tom's Maternal
  Grandmother... xxi
Photo 9: Rowena L. Thyng, 1823–1911, Rachel's Paternal
  Grandmother xxii
Photo 10: George N. Shepard, 1824–1903, Rachel's Paternal
  Grandfather xxii
Photo 11: Tom in Typical Baby Clothes of the Day 1
Photo 12: Mabel, James Maxwell, and Grandma Caroline Higgins 2
Photo 13: Jay P. in College, ca. 1890s 2
Photo 14: Mabel (left) with Her Half-Sister, Ida Palmer, and
  Half-Brother, John Palmer 3
Photo 15: Higgins Family Gathering 4

Photo 16: Tom (1st row, 2nd from right) with His Second-Grade Class ... 5
Photo 17: Tom (with crossed arms) and His Third-Grade Class 6
Photo 18: Tom (back row, 4th from left) with His Fourth-Grade Class 6
Photo 19: Birdie Frasier, Dad's Teacher, with Tom and Max 7
Photo 20: The "Shack" 8
Photo 21: A Stylized Drawing of T. T. Higgins's Farm by an
Unknown Artist 9
Photo 22: Tom in a Dowagiac Band Uniform at Age 12 10
Photo 23: Tom, Age 17 (back row, 2nd from left) with the Niles
High School Orchestra 11
Photo 24: Tom Sitting on a Fence with a Friend............................. 12
Photo 25: Tom (holding trumpet) with Two Other M.A.C. Musicians ... 13
Photo 26: First-Year Students in the Agricultural Program at M.A.C. ... 14
Photo 27: Tom with Dog in New Hampshire, ca. 1923 15
Photo 28: The Pearsons' Home in the 1920s 17
Photo 29: Tom Standing on Six Feet of Snow 18
Photo 30: Tom (holding trumpet) with Other Band Members 20
Photo 31: Tom (on the left) with Friends 21
Photo 32: Tom in a Reserve Officers' Training Corps (ROTC)
Uniform, ca. 1925.. 22
Photo 33: University of New Hampshire Band (Tom is on the
far right in the 2nd row) 23
Photo 34: Rachel's Home in West Epping 26
Photo 35: Herman T. Shepard, ca. 1888 27
Photo 36: A Group Gathering with Herman T. Shepard, ca. 1890s
(Herman is 3rd from the left in the back row) 29
Photo 37: Rose Shepard in a Nurse's Uniform 30
Photo 38: Rose Shepard, Age 44, with Rachel, Age 5 31
Photo 39: Rachel, Age 8, with George, Age 4 31
Photo 40: Rachel (far right) at York Beach, Maine, ca. 1926............... 32
Photo 41: Rachel (sitting behind the child) at York Beach, Maine,
ca. 1926 33
Photo 42: Rachel (2nd from right) at York Beach, Maine, ca. 1926 33
Photo 43: Rachel, ca. 1920s 34

List of Photos

Photo 44: Ching Foh Bau and Tom, ca. 1927 37
Photo 45: Rachel in Her Graduation Gown, 1927 37
Photo 46: Rachel, ca. the Late 1920s 38
Photo 47: Tom on His Wedding Day, February 5, 1928 39
Photo 48: The Cassopolis Community Band (Tom is 4th from
 the left in the back row) 41
Photo 49: Interior of Tom and Rachel's Cottage, ca. 1955 44
Photo 50: Nine Gables 45
Photo 51: Lorol Schopflocher, ca. 1920s 47
Photo 52: The Main Street of Kingston As It Is Today
 (The building in the foreground is the former post office) 50
Photo 53: A Plaque Showing the Original Name of Kingston 51
Photo 54: Rachel at Sunny Ridge Farm, ca. 1929 53
Photo 55: Rachel in a Car at Sunny Ridge Farm, ca. 1929................. 53
Photo 56: East Farm, ca. 1931 57
Photo 57: The Sign at the Entrance to East Farm, 2024 58
Photo 58: The Egg-Laying Contest Building, ca. 1950 59
Photo 59: The Gough Farmhouse with Nancy Standing in Front,
 ca. 2020 (It looked much the same when she was a girl)............... 60
Photo 60: The Gough Farmhouse As Seen from the Back, 2024 60
Photo 61: The Poultry Department Office Building, 2024
 (which is now used by the East Farm Trout Research Facility) 61
Photo 62: Playbill for "The Return of Peter Grimm," Presented by
 the Kingston Players.. 62
Photo 63: Larry at 1 Year Old 63
Photo 64: Mom and Larry at the Beach, ca. 1933 64
Photo 65: Mom and Dad at Christmastime, ca. 1930s 65
Photo 66: Larry, Age 4, in Front of a Chicken Coop 66
Photo 67: Dad, Larry, Mom, and the Twins, ca. 1937 67
Photo 68: Larry and the Twins, ca. 1938 67
Photo 69: Teresa and Nancy in Jammies, 1938 68
Photo 70: Larry Wearing a Suit That Dad Had Made for Him 68
Photo 71: Nancy, Larry, Mom, and Teresa (in front of Great-Grandpa
 Shepard's Farmhouse, West Epping, New Hampshire, ca. 1939) ... 69

Photo 72: One of Dad's Batiks, ca. Late 1930s 70
Photo 73: Sef-Portrait of Dad, ca. 1930s 71
Photo 74: Plaster Cast of Larry's Head, ca. 1938 72
Photo 75: Wooden Tray with Nude Handles, ca. 1940s 73
Photo 76: "The Vintage" by Julius Ralshoven 74
Photo 77: Dad's 12.5" x 18" Copy of "The Vintage" 75
Photo 78: East Farm Poultry Department Staff, ca. 1940 (Left to right, standing in front of the Poultry Department office building: unidentified farmhand, Ray Taylor, Stanley Smith, Dr. John Delaplane, Prudy Robinson, Homer Stuart, Tom Higgins, and two other unidentified farmhands) 78
Photo 79: Dr. John Weldin and Dad Examining Chickens, ca. 1940 78
Photo 80: One of the Former Poultry Buildings on East Farm, 2024...... 79
Photo 81: Green Hall, Which Housed the University Library and Administrative Offices, 1939.. 79
Photo 82: Larry's Model of Holy Trinity Monastery, 1947 (from the Holy Trinity Monastery and Seminary Photo Collection) 84
Photo 83: Holy Trinity Monastery, Jordanville, New York, 1948 84
Photo 84: An Ad During World War II 86
Photo 85: Mary Endo and Her Brothers, ca. 1950s 87
Photo 86: The Demonstration Vegetable Garden, 2024 89
Photo 87: View from the Master Gardener's Field House at East Farm... 90
Photo 88: The Quonset Hut As It Looked in 2024 94
Photo 89: Dad Candling Eggs, ca. 1940 95
Photo 90: Some of the East Farm Staff, ca. Late 1940s 96
Photo 91: The Horticultural Building Where Teresa and Nancy Found Casks of Cider 97
Photo 92: The House in Usquepaug 101
Photo 93: Dad's Graduation Day, May 28, 1944 106
Photo 94: The Local South County Orchestra, ca. 1940s (Dad is standing at the far right, with May Steadman to his left and Dean Royal Wales in front with a cello) 109
Photo 95: Mom, Teresa, Nancy, and Larry, ca. 1946 (Dad made Larry's suit and the twins' treasured corduroy Eisenhower jackets) 112
Photo 96: Teresa and Nancy with Mary Endo, ca. 1940s 113

List of Photos

Photo 97: Dad (on the left) and Dr. Delaplane Inoculating a Chicken ... 114
Photo 98: A Family Picnic in Our Backyard with Dr. and Mrs. Delaplane (standing between Mom and Dad, and the Delaplane girls are seated on either side of the twins) 115
Photo 99: Mom and Dad Cooking a Chicken on a Spit 116
Photo 100: A Fruit Growers' Meeting at East Farm, ca. 1930 117
Photo 101: Nancy, Teresa, and Larry at Gettysburg 119
Photo 102: Teresa and Nancy Wearing Their New Suits (across from the Kingston Congregational Church) 120
Photo 103: Dad's Clothing Label 121
Photo 104: Teresa, Mom, Larry, and Nancy (Note the low ceiling in the living room and the twins' suits made by Dad 121
Photo 105: Larry's Mighty Moe's Ice Cream Truck, ca. 1955 122
Photo 106: Dad Dousing with a Tree Branch Near the House 125
Photo 107: The Rhode Island Red 126
Photo 108: My Rhode Island Red Pin... 127
Photo 109: Our New Home, Dad's Pride and Joy 130
Photo 110: Dad Tending to the Fireplace, 1965 131
Photo 111: My Senior Project, a Handwoven Bedspread 132
Photo 112: Dad Holding Nancy's Daughter, Christine, in 1967........... 136
Photo 113: A Cartoon by Paule Loring of Dad and Violet Higbee Barbecuing 137
Photo 114: Dad and Mom, ca. 1974 139
Photo 115: Dad (far right), ca. 1964 142
Photo 116: Dad's Official Retirement Photo 144
Photo 117: Dad Barbecuing on a Camping Trip, ca. 1968 145
Photo 118: Dad Painting in His Studio, ca. 1970 146
Photo 119: Dad Painting in His Studio, ca. 1971 147
Photo 120: Pastel of Jesse Leon Witkoe and Nancy Lyn Hathaway, ca. 1982 148
Photo 121: Oil Painting of Christine Shepard Hall, 1976 149
Photo 122: Oil Painting of Camille Higgins, 1981 149
Photo 123: Watercolor of Patricia Ann Hathaway, 1977 150
Photo 124: The Pottery Studio in the Former Kingston Post Office 151

Photo 125: Painting of Becky Rafanello 152
Photo 126: Photograph of Becky Rafanello 153
Photo 127: Dad Admiring His Painting of Janice Thibedault 153
Photo 128: Dad at a Private Showing of His Paintings 154
Photo 129: Dad and Mom in San Francisco, 1984 157
Photo 130: Mom (on the left) with Shirley Chisholm, Former
    Congresswoman from New York (on the right) 157
Photo 131: Dad and Mom (on the left) with Fellow Peace
    Activists Almena and Ted Neff 158
Photo 132: Teresa and Mom, Age 95, 2001 159
Photo 133: Oil Painting of Janice Thibedault 166
Photo 134: Portrait 167
Photo 135: Still Life 168
Photo 136: Still Life, 1989 169
Photo 137: Still Life, 1967 170
Photo 138: Still Life 171
Photo 139: Still Life 172
Photo 140: Portrait 173
Photo 141: Landscape 174
Photo 142: Landscape 175
Photo 143: Still Life 176
Photo 144: Still Life 177
Photo 145: Portrait 178
Photo 146: Portrait, 1975 179
Photo 147: Landscape 180
Photo 148: Landscape 181
Photo 149: Nude 182
Photo 150: Nude 183
Photo 151: Portrait 184
Photo 152: Portrait 185
Photo 153: Portrait 186
Photo 154: Portrait 187
Photo 155: Nude 188
Photo 156: Portrait of Janice Thibedault 189

List of Photos

Photo 157: Nude 190
Photo 158: Nude 191
Photo 159: Nude 192
Photo 160: Nude 193
Photo 161: Portrait 194
Photo 162: Portrait, 1966 195
Photo 163: Nude 196
Photo 164: Nude 197
Photo 165: Portrait 198
Photo 166: Portrait 199
Photo 167: Portrait 200
Photo 168: Becky 201
Photo 169: Nude 202
Photo 170: Nude 203
Photo 171: Portrait 204
Photo 172: Portrait 205
Photo 173: Portrait 206
Photo 174: Portrait 207
Photo 175: Portrait of Patricia Ann Hathaway, 1977 208
Photo 176: Portrait of Cindy, 1977 209
Photo 177: Nude 210
Photo 178: Nude 211
Photo 179: Nude 212
Photo 180: Nude 213
Photo 181: Portrait of Rose Etta Shepard, 1980 214
Photo 182: Portrait 215
Photo 183: Landscape 216
Photo 184: Landscape 217
Photo 185: Portrait 218
Photo 186: Portrait of Janice Thibedault... 219
Photo 187: Portrait of Thomas C. Higgins, ca. 1972, by Herman
  Itchkawich 220

A Tribute

You gentle me,
my brash uneven ways
call into question
what I think is love
and summon from some secret place
the tenderness I had forgot was there.
To be with you
defines the verb to be.
Because of you
I am myself the more.

Rachel Shepard Higgins (1906–2006)
Autumn Crocus, Anniversary Edition*

**Autumn Crocus* was a booklet of poetry that my mother wrote ca. 1989.

Preface

When my mother was approaching her hundredth year, I decided to republish her small book of poems, *Autumn Crocus*, which included some family history and photos. In a way, that was the genesis for this book, which has grown far beyond my initial intentions. I attempt to tell here the story of my father from farm boy to artist, an endeavor that has been most challenging and enlightening. I found that I loved the research, digging for pieces of information and finding tidbits here and there.

My father started married life as a farmer, went on to advise other farmers, and then proceeded to teach future farmers. In the early years of his marriage, he pursued many art interests, but it was in retirement that his passion for art grew.

It has been a long effort for me to put all the pieces together—almost ten years. My primary focus for this book has been to provide a record of my father's artistic work. My brother, sister, and I own a number of his pieces, but some are in unknown locations or lost. Because there were slides of many of his portraits, particularly the nudes, I was able to use those photos in this book.

My father was very talented in many areas, and I hope I shed a little light on his life for readers to enjoy. I only wish I had asked more questions when my parents were alive.

In a local *Narragansett Times* newspaper article by Arnold W. Peterson, dated September 28, 1990, my father was called a "twentieth-century Renaissance man" because he experimented with painting, sculpting, woodcarving, pottery, batiks, and gardening. He also enjoyed taking photographs, especially of his children. He played the trumpet from early school days until the 1950s. When I was a child, I thought he could do just about anything—all the typical farm activities from gardening to raising animals to maintaining our old farmhouse. He could repair all manner of things—and did. He wallpapered, painted, and enlarged the living room in our house. I learned so much from watching him and became quite handy myself.

He also sewed—first, I think, making a "Sunday go to church suit" for my brother, Larry. He made another suit when Larry went off to prep school at Mt. Hermon in Gill, Massachusetts. Then he made identical Eisenhower-style jackets for my twin sister, Teresa, and me from a dark brown corduroy fabric. We treasured those jackets. World War II had recently ended, and General Eisenhower was still a hero. Later, Dad made tan tweed woolen suits and shoulder bags from soft leather. Nobody else's dad could beat that. He reupholstered furniture as needed and made draperies. The sewing was probably an economic necessity for him, but also, I presume, a satisfying artistic challenge. My mother, on the other hand, wasn't much of a seamstress.

I have included in the following pages some genealogical information from both sides of my family. The first page includes names of great-grandparents and great-great grandparents of whom there are no known photographs. Following those are several photos of ancestors on the Higgins side and two on the Shepard side.

Ancestors Without Photos

Tom's Ancestors

Gideon A. Palmer
1804–1882
Tom's Maternal Great-Grandfather

Margaret Jane Creelman
1803–1876
Tom's Maternal Great-Grandmother

James Wiley
1807–1890
Tom's Maternal Great-Grandfather

Mary Ellen Poole
1821–1895
Tom's Maternal Great-Grandmother

Rachel's Ancestors

Samuel Shepard
1798–1834
Rachel's Paternal Great-Grandfather

Hannah Norris
1804–?
Rachel's Paternal Great-Grandmother

Dudley Thyng
1806–1878
Rachel's Paternal Great-Grandfather

Elizabeth Durgin
1804–?
Rachel's Paternal Great-Grandmother

Charles F. Smith
1813–1863
Rachel's Maternal Great-Grandfather

Judith H. Cram
1817–?
Rachel's Maternal Great-Grandmother

Leslie Haynes
?–?
Rachel's Maternal Grandfather

Susan Minerva Smith
1845–1909
Rachel's Maternal Grandmother

Photo 1: James T. Higgins
1807–1898
Tom's Paternal Great-Grandfather

Photo 2: Mary A. Higgins
1813–1872
Tom's Paternal Great-Grandmother

Preface

Photo 3: Lucius Rathbun
1800–1875
Tom's Paternal Great-Grandfather

Photo 4: Sarah Glick
1813–1891
Tom's Paternal Great-Grandmother

Photo 5: Thomas Titus Higgins
1844–1916
Tom's Paternal Grandfather

Photo 6: Caroline Rathbun
1846–1934
Tom's Paternal Grandmother

Preface

Photo 7: Samuel Nathaniel Palmer
1829–1898
Tom's Maternal Grandfather

Photo 8: Margaret E. Wiley
1841–1914
Tom's Maternal Grandmother

Photo 9: Rowena L. Thyng
1823–1911
Rachel's Paternal Grandmother

Photo 10: George N. Shepard
1824–1903
Rachel's Paternal Grandfather

Chapter 1:
Tom's Early Years

My father, Thomas Craven Higgins, the son of Jay P. (who went by the initials J. P.) and Mabel Palmer Higgins, was born on January 18, 1902, probably in Detroit, Michigan. As a little boy, he was called Craven, but he never liked that name, and became Tom or Thomas sometime in elementary school. Shortly after he was born, the family moved to Halstad Street in Dowagiac, Michigan, a small town of about 4,200 people, where they lived for the next fourteen years. His brother, James Maxwell Higgins, was born on September 28, 1904.

Photo 11: Tom in Typical Baby Clothes of the Day

Photo 12: Mabel, James Maxwell, and Grandma Caroline Higgins, ca. 1904

To go back in time a bit, Tom's father, Jay P., was born in 1870, attended Michigan State Normal School in Ypsilanti, and became a teacher.

Photo 13: Jay P. in College, ca. 1890s

Marriage Gone Awry

Jay P. was first married in 1895 to his high-school sweetheart, Nettie Savage, the love of his life. They both attended school in Ypsilanti and became teachers. Their one child, Janeth, born in 1897, did not survive the year. I'm not sure if Tom ever knew about the baby, since he never mentioned it. Perhaps the loss of a child destroyed Jay P.'s marriage, for Nettie divorced him in 1899, an unthinkable event at that time. Tom said that Jay P. never fully recovered from the divorce. It was only from divorce records that I even learned about the child. From the 1900 Census, it appears that Jay P. moved to Detroit in that year and worked as a sawyer at a sawmill. Nettie's brother, a close friend of Jay P.'s, often visited him in the following years, which would reignite Jay P.'s depression.

Second Time Around

Fortunately, Jay P. soon met Mabel Palmer, who was 19 and twelve years his junior. She was from Canada, and I suspect that she was visiting her relatives, the Wileys, in Cass County, Michigan, at the time. The couple married in Tilbury, Canada, on July 3, 1901. Dad described his mother as always ready to laugh, always honest, and always even-handed with everybody. I suppose you could say the same about him.

Photo 14: Mabel (left) with Her Half-Sister, Ida Palmer, and Half-Brother, John

Photo 15: Higgins Family Gathering[1]

Like many young people today, Jay P. was involved in several occupations over the years, but never seemed to find his niche. In a letter to my sister in 1976, Dad described his father as a brilliant and gifted man, but not much of a husband, provider, or father. In 1886, at age 16, Jay P. taught elementary school. Twenty-four years later, in 1910, he became a newspaper reporter, and then sold insurance and real estate, and worked in telephone communications. When his father died, he reluctantly became a farmer. In a 1945 letter to Jay P., Dad wrote of how proud he had been to have his own father as his teacher, adding at the end, "I have said you were about the best schoolteacher I ever had."

The city of Dowagiac, Michigan, was named after Chief Dowagiac,

---

[1] *Left to right front row:* Philip Shurter, Lynn Shurter, Thomas C. Higgins, Zed Atlee, James Maxwell Higgins. *Left to right back row:* Claude Higgins, Thomas T. Higgins, Mrs. Caroline Higgins, Jay P. Higgins, Elsie Higgins Atlee, Florence Higgins Shurter, Leona Gifford Higgins (Claude's wife), Frederick Shurter (Florence's husband), Mabel Palmer Higgins (Jay P. Higgins's wife).

a Potawatomi Indian. As Tom was growing up, his playmates were whites, blacks, and a couple of Indian boys. Tom wrote that that was a happy time for him. The father of one of the Indian boys was the chief of the local Potawatomi tribe, a handsome six-footer and superintendent of the Dowagiac Drill Company, which manufactured grain drills and other farm implements.

Inescapable Schooling

In what was a common practice in the early twentieth century, Tom's teacher at Dowagiac's McKinley Grammar School, Birdie Frazier, roomed with his family for ten years, sleeping in my father's bedroom. I assume they had separate beds, but I wonder how that affected Dad emotionally. As an adult, he was very comfortable with women and had many female friends.

In a note on the back of a picture of Dad's third-grade class at the school, he wrote that this was a particularly mischievous period for him. I wonder in what way. In Photo 17, he does have a rather cocky look about him.

Photo 16: Tom (1st row, 2nd from right) with His Second-Grade Class

Photo 17: Tom (middle of 3rd row with crossed arms) and His Third-Grade Class[2]

Photo 18: Tom (back row, 4th from left) with His Fourth-Grade Class

---

[2]Birdie Frazier, Tom's teacher, is at the back on the right.

My dad and his brother, Max, must have had a very close relationship with Birdie Frazier, because she apparently promised to leave her home to the two of them in her will. Dad later tried to find the probate of her will, but was unsuccessful. I suspect he was interested in the financial aspects. Below, we have a wonderful photo of the trio. This looks like a family photo, but it is not.

Photo 19: Birdie Frazier, Dad's Teacher, with Max and Tom

Photo 20: The "Shack"

Jay P. liked to write poetry, and in later years he wrote a poem for Tom describing the "Shack" as having no electricity, no running water, no telephone, and no toilet. The furniture was all secondhand, with rag carpets on the floor and a horseshoe over the door. In the poem, Jay P. further wrote of the Shack, "There was heaps of sunshine in it to drive the gloominess away." He ended the poem by saying that Mother could always see the dark clouds' silver lining.

Tom's Grandpa

Dad often talked of having a happy childhood, with his cousins, Lynn and Phil Shurter and Zed Atlee, living nearby. Another cousin, Orleta Whitmore, lived with Dad's grandparents, Thomas T. and Caroline Higgins, on their farm in Jefferson Township, Michigan, about fifteen miles from Dowagiac. Dad's grandfather, who was active in local politics, was elected to the Michigan State Legislature for two terms, beginning in 1903. Previous to that, he was Deputy State Inspector of Oils under Governor Cyrus G. Luce. In a 1906 biographical sketch of Thomas T. Higgins, he is described as being thoroughly reliable in his business transactions, his name being synonymous with integrity and straightforward dealing.³ He was a prosperous farmer, who grew wheat, Indian corn, and oats on 200 acres of cultivated land. The farm had the usual variety of livestock: horses, dairy cows, beef cattle, pigs, and chickens. In a letter to my sister, my dad wrote:

> *Grandpa was my hero. In the newspaper, he was referred to as Honorable, but to his friends and neighbors as Honest Tom. Dad went on to describe seeing his grandfather, at age seventy and six-feet-four, throw and castrate a 500-pound boar. They didn't need him for breeding purposes, so they "altered" him. Gramp didn't know I was peeking. I was a little kid. There I stood, bug-eyed and a little sick at the sight, the squealing, and blood. But I never forgot it. The boar was mean and had chased me once. Perhaps that is why Gramp decided to tame him, and send him to market.*

*Photo 21: A Stylized Drawing of Thomas T. Higgins's Farm by an Unknown Artist*⁴

Dad said that the farm was located in a tornado path, and during one high windstorm the neighbor's barn doors actually flew over the house and landed in the barnyard. There was no damage, but plenty of excitement. Dad spent summers at the farm and said that his cousin

---

³L. H. Glover, ed. *A Twentieth-Century History of Cass County, Michigan* (Chicago and New York: Lewis Publishing Company, 1906), pp. 409–412.
⁴Anonymous, *History of Cass County, Michigan* (Chicago: Waterman, Watkins & Co., 1882), facing p. 380. Available at https://www.loc.gov/item/01007013/.

Orleta, who was two years younger, could hold her own in a tussle. While she was willful, he said, she was smart, with nothing mean about her. He remembered with humor the time he was sitting out back, when she came out with a bucket of sudsy water and a mop with directions from Grandma Caroline to wash the stoop. About this incident, he wrote to me in a letter:

> *She asked me to move, and I just sat there looking unconcerned. When Orleta asked me again to move, and I didn't, Wham, I had the full force of that wet, dripping mop wrapped around my face and neck! I moved.*

Dad's grandfather, Thomas T. Higgins, died on May 26, 1916, at age 72. That must have been a huge blow for my dad. Grandma Caroline was now alone and needed help. I would guess that Jay P., Mabel, and the boys moved from Dowagiac to the family homestead in Jefferson Township that year. I know it was not Jay P.'s desire to become a farmer, and according to Dad he was not a very hard worker. Dad was 14 at the time and a newsboy during World War I.

Photo 22: Tom in a Dowagiac High School Band Uniform at Age 12

Dad attended Dowagiac High School, and then Niles High School in Jefferson Township after he moved to the farm. I have a photo of him wearing the Dowagiac High School Band uniform, as well as another photo of him in the Niles High School Orchestra.

Photo 23: Tom, Age 17 (back row, 2nd from left) with the Niles High School Orchestra

There is no record of his graduation, and his schooling was apparently disrupted at times when he lived at the farm. My brother believes that Dad dropped out of high school to help his father on the farm. That was certainly news to me. Since he was such a proponent of education, I imagine he never wanted us to know that. So far as I know, he was not active in school sports, but participated in the music programs.

After I sent Dad a Wynton Marsalis phonograph record on his 87th birthday, he wrote:

> *I have enjoyed the record so much. Wynton Marsalis is wonderful on the trumpet, and the music reminded me of the*

wonderful circus bands when I was a child. When a kid at the circus, I always tried to sit near the band, for they were in those days artists. I recall the leader of the Ringling Circus who played cornet. He played the lead solos of much of the music that Marsalis plays on the recording. I was spellbound and forgot for the moment the high-wire acrobat on the bike.

Dad played the trumpet in numerous bands, including the high school band, when he was only 12. His brother, Max, was also musical and sang in local choirs, later training to be a soloist.

Tom's First Ride from Horse to Horsepower

In a 1990 newspaper article, Dad was quoted as saying that transportation during his childhood was primarily by horse and buggy:

I learned to drive a Ford back in the days when few people were driving at all. The automobile company that was selling cars said to my father, "Send Tom up." I'd never driven before. I went up with horse and buggy and came back with a Model T. As long as you were driving in the ruts, you were all right.[5]

Photo 24: Tom Sitting on a Fence with a Friend

---

[5]Arnold W. Peterson, "Tom Higgins, a 20th-Century Renaissance Man," *Narragansett Times*, September 28, 1990, pp. 3A and 10A.

At that time, around 1917, many of the roads were unpaved, so they were rutted or grooved by horses and buggies, wagons, or farm machinery, creating a very bumpy ride. What a thrill that must have been!

Raising a Pig Can Change Your Life

In 1920, Dad was a farm boy destined to become a young farmer. At the age of 18, he won a Boys and Girls Club agricultural contest for raising a Belted Hampshire pig, beating out fifty other boys in the county. That breed of pig has a black body with a white band around the middle and down the front legs. Since my great-grandfather, who owned the farm, usually raised one or two pigs, I suspect that Dad chose a special one to groom for the contest. When he won that contest, he received a scholarship for a sixteen-week short course in agricultural studies at Michigan Agricultural College, or M.A.C. as it was known at the time, later becoming Michigan State University. The course included Animal Feeding, Farm Crops, Agricultural Chemistry, Study of Breeds, Disease Control, Horticulture, and more. The scholarship that Dad won covered the first year of a two-year college program.

Photo 25: Tom (on left, holding trumpet) with Two Other M.A.C. Musicians

Dad attended Michigan Agricultural College during the 1921–1922 school year. When he arrived on campus, he roomed with a World War I veteran, who was the superintendent of a farm in Hart, Michigan.

Photo 26: First-Year Students in the Agriculture Program at M.A.C.[6]

---

[6]Photos 15 and 16 are from the *Wolverine* yearbook of 1922, Michigan Agricultural College, University Archives and Historical Collections, Michigan State University Yearbooks, pp. 248 and 254. Tom is in the 3rd row, 2nd from the right.

The sixteen-week short course introduced Dad to college life and to people who inspired him to continue his education. True to form, he quickly became a member of the M.A.C. Orchestra.

In a letter he wrote to my sister, Teresa, in 1978, he said, "That changed my life, I had a taste of college." Although his father, Jay P., had attended college and taught school, he had not encouraged Dad to continue his schooling because, according to Dad, he "didn't approve of college education for a boy who wanted to be a farmer."[7] I suppose that's why he was unable to pursue his education at M.A.C. Money may also have been an issue. If I had been in his shoes, I would have been devastated. It wasn't long before Dad decided to leave home.

Photo 27: Tom with Dog in New Hampshire, ca. 1923

---

[7]Peterson, "Tom Higgins," pp. 3A and 10A.

Chapter 2:
Traveling East

Tom was apparently adventuresome and ambitious, so, not long after attending M.A.C., he traveled east, working at lumber camps along the way. When he arrived in New Hampshire, he stayed with his former roommate, the World War I veteran from Michigan. Through him, Dad met Frank Pearson from Stratham, a market gardener who sold produce to local stores. When Tom walked from town out to Pearson's farm, looking for a job, Pearson hired him on the spot. He must have been impressed by the go-get-'em-ness of the adventurous young man.

Photo 28: The Pearsons' Home in the 1920s

When Tom arrived that winter, there were six feet of snow on the ground, so there wouldn't have been much gardening to do, but many chores, from sawing wood, to pruning trees, to shoveling snow and hauling ice. One day, Frank and Tom hauled in 112 cakes of ice with Frank's truck. It took them all day to pack those huge blocks and then cover them with sawdust.

Photo 29: Tom Standing on Six Feet of Snow, ca. 1923

Traveling East

Tom worked for Frank Pearson and lived with his family for two years, beginning in March 1923. Frank and his wife, Grace, treated Tom as a son. When Tom moved in, the couple already had one son, Oscar (who was 21), and three daughters: Dorothy (19), Margaret (16), and Georgiana (13). I like to think I was named after Georgiana, whose nickname was Nan. Dad always talked fondly of her.

Oscar Pearson wrote in his memoir:

> *One winter day a young fellow, Tom Higgins, walked in thru the Whitcomb pasture [which was adjacent to the Pearson property], and spent several years with us. He came from Michigan, and wanted to attend New Hampshire State College at Durham, but needed money. Dad took him on to pick up the chores I dropped when I moved to Durham. We were within a couple of days of being the same age. He was headed for Durham, too, but needed to save up enough to get started and also to establish residence in New Hampshire....*
>
> *I usually spent the weekends at home, playing the sax with Tom. He was so much more a musician than I was. We worked up a band and organized dances in the Town Hall. I've forgotten who played the drums, or even if we had any, but Dot sometimes played the piano, or we would get Louise Smith from Exeter, who could really belt it out. I had to furnish transportation for her, usually the Ford light truck with one of the floorboards out, and she arrived fully windblown. She didn't like it much, but $5 was real money then.*[8]

I'm amazed that Dad never mentioned these experiences of playing in a band at dances—especially since my husband, Don, is a musician, who has played at dances for the last seven decades. You would think there might have been a little connection there.

Oscar attended New Hampshire State College (later the University of New Hampshire) and traveled by train every day to the campus in Durham. He later moved to Durham to pursue his studies. In his sister Margaret's diary, she mentions Tom almost daily as participating in the family's social events, as well as walking to the post office in town each

---

[8]Oscar Pearson, *The Stratham Farm*, p. 18, Tate Box 1 (91.7.34), Stratham Historical Society, Stratham, New Hampshire, 1985.

day with her or one of her sisters. At that time, mail was delivered to the post office twice a day, but there was no home delivery.

Photo 30: Tom (holding trumpet) with Other Band Members

Margaret worked at the Robinson Female Seminary in Exeter, New Hampshire, from which she had graduated in 1924. The school, which was modeled after Philips Exeter Academy for boys, was founded in 1867. Margaret worked at the school, recording grades, sending out tuition notices, typing, and generally filling in as needed. On one very snowy day, Dorothy, Margaret's older sister, who was also a graduate of the Seminary, hitched up a two-horse sled and went to the school with friends to take all the children home. What a delight that must have been!

Social events included church every Sunday morning, followed by other events in the evening. These were often slideshows or talks about various countries around the world. One night, there was a stereopticon lecture on Japan. The stereopticon was a type of slide projector that combined two images to create a three-dimensional effect. There were also whist card parties, a precursor to bridge, as well as minstrel shows and plays at the town hall. Outdoor events included skiing, sledding, snowshoeing, jumping rope, or playing "Peggy." The last of these was a once-popular children's game played with an old broom handle and a small rectangular block, or peg, that had tapered ends. The peg, or "Peggy," was placed on the ground and hit with the broom handle on the pointed end. The player had three attempts to hit the Peggy as it flew up in the air. I can just imagine that challenging game. Tom participated in all of those events.

Photo 31: Tom (on the left) with friends

Tom's Ticket to the Future

One day during the second summer, Mr. Pearson took Tom aside and said, "Tom you should go back to college. I can get you a scholarship at the University of New Hampshire."

Tom accepted the offer, moved to Durham in January 1925, and enrolled in the Agriculture Two-Year Course at the University.⁹ From Margaret's diary, I learned that Tom found a room in town with Frank Hobbs, presumably a fellow student, as well as a part-time job in Fremont.¹⁰ Tuition at that time for residents was fifty dollars a year, and general fees were thirty-five dollars.¹¹ That first year, Tom joined Alpha Tau Alpha fraternity, an organization for two-year students. Military training was required, as can be seen in the photo below.

Photo 32: Tom in a Reserve Officers' Training Corps (ROTC) Uniform, ca. 1925

⁹University of New Hampshire. *Two-Year Course in Agriculture*, Bulletin of the University of New Hampshire, vol. 17, issue 2 (1925).

¹⁰Margaret Pearson, diary, January 6, 1925 and April 8, 1925, Stratham Historical Society, Stratham, NH.

¹¹University of New Hampshire, *Two-Year Course in Agriculture*.

Taking a Different Path: The Lure of the Farm

Tom completed the first year of the program, but something changed his educational plans, since he didn't continue his studies the second year. At least, I can find no documentation that he continued. Perhaps the offer of a job at the university's poultry plant seemed more desirable. Tom spoke of being the foreman at the farm during the 1927–1928 school year, during which he lived on campus. In a letter to his mother, dated February 9, 1927, he wrote:

> *I am going to build a poultry building, 24' x 30' for pedigree work with the help of students taking poultry house construction. Hatch about ten thousand chickens, [and] five thousand of them we are going to raise. The other five we shall sell.*

Tom had just turned 25 and was entrusted with enormous responsibilities. What a lot of challenges for a young man to tackle! He would return to the farm in Stratham on most weekends with Oscar, who was a graduate student at the time. From Margaret's diary, I learned that Tom and Oscar took the train from Durham to Exeter, which was about three miles from Stratham.

Photo 33: University of New Hampshire Band
(Tom is on the far right in the 2nd row)

The train ran directly through the campus, as it does to this day. In fact, the University of New Hampshire now owns the station. As weekend commuters, they missed out on many of the campus activities, but enjoyed dances, card parties, plays, and other activities in Stratham. However, Tom didn't pass up the chance to play with the University of New Hampshire Band.

Chapter 3:
A Blind Date

Tom met his future wife, Rachel E. Shepard, from West Epping, New Hampshire, on a blind date. She was majoring in French at New Hampshire State College, inspired by seeing French-language newspapers and dictionary pages pasted on the walls of the privy at her childhood home. In her 80s, she wrote about this in her journal:

> One day in 1914, I was 8 years old. I was sitting on the little "hole out back" reading the page I had put on the wall. It was written in French and said in part "Ces lettres chez nous," and a long paragraph in French. I found a dictionary with French words and phrases in the back. I deciphered some of the words. It is a letter from a French soldier to his folks back home [during World War I]. It makes me weep. My first love, French.

Those pages acted as a type of insulation to keep the wind out, but their contents seemed exotic and enchanting to her. There were many French Canadians in the area, and hence the French-language papers.

Rachel lived in what would be called a duplex today, and the privy, a "three-holer" at the back of the house, was shared by two families. A shared water pump was also at the back of the house. There were no modern conveniences while Rachel lived there. However, the Folsoms, who lived in the other half of the house, upgraded their side of the house when utilities became available, but the Shepards did not.

An Adventurous Minister

Rachel's father, Herman Thyng Shepard, graduated from Harvard University and Andover Theological Seminary sometime between 1891 and 1894. He was an itinerant Congregational minister in mining camps in Montana, South Dakota, and Washington. I would call him a liberal of the times, preaching for miners' rights. Named after his mother, he didn't like his middle name and often used the name Herman Thomas Shepard instead.

Photo 34: Rachel's Home in West Epping

From a scrapbook containing newspaper accounts of his sermons from Butte, Montana, I found that he preached on many topics, including miners, newspapers, and the theatre. He was adamantly opposed to drinking, gambling, and dance hall saloons. A Seattle newspaper from April 1893 reported that Rev. H. T. Shepard's home was burned to the ground in Black Diamond, Washington. Family lore intimates that the fire may have been set in retaliation for his support of miners' rights. In trying to save his valuable library, he was scorched about the hands and face.[12]

---

[12]"Pastor Shepard's House Burned," *Seattle Post-Intelligencer*, vol. 23, no. 144 (April 7, 1893), p. 5.

Photo 35: Herman T. Shepard, ca. 1888

Fighting Debauchery

A year later, in 1894, Herman preached against a saloon that was associated with a dance hall in Black Diamond, Washington. Feelings ran high in town, and the license was revoked. A month later, Shepard was physically involved in removing a Mrs. Morgan from the barroom. It is quite a convoluted tale, and I don't really know who owned the bar, or "dive" as it was called. There may have been living quarters at the site, which is why the story mentions a bed and cribs:

> *Morgan and his wife still held her bed in the barroom and defied all bands to put her out. Isaac P. Calhoun, H. T. Shepard, and Mr. Morgan pulled off their coats and leveled the woman's cribs to the ground and burned them.*[13]

Perhaps that is putting into practice what you preach? In the same article, it is said that threats were made on the life of Shepard by the "dive men." The term *dive* was first used in the 1880s to describe disreputable places where alcohol was served, quite often in basements. The dive men alluded to in the newspaper were probably patrons of the bar. Perhaps Herman's next move was precipitated by those events.

On the Move Again

In October of 1894, Shepard moved to Butte, Montana, where he became pastor of the Congregational Church for about one year. From there he moved to Elk Point, South Dakota, and finally, in 1897, to San Francisco, where he became pastor of the Olivet Congregational Church at 17th and Noe Streets. In 1901, his budding career was cut short when he resigned to return home to West Epping, to take care of his aging parents and to help his father with the family businesses, which I believe included a general store and a coal business. Herman's ministerial career had ended, which I suppose was a bitter pill for him. His father, George N. Shepard, a Civil War hero, died two years later, in 1903. It is said that he was so respected that the bells of all the churches in town were rung.

---

[13]"The Dive Is Now Deserted," *Seattle Post-Intelligencer*, vol. 25, no. 147 (April 13, 1894), p. 5.

*Photo 36: A Group Gathering with Herman T. Shepard, ca. 1890s
(Herman is 3rd from the left in the back row)*

Romance Blooms

When Herman's mother, Rowena Shepard, became ill, Herman hired Rose Etta Smith, a nurse, to help her. They fell in love and were married on May 6, 1905. Rachel was born the following year on April 14, 1906. In 1911, Rowena passed away, and a year later Rachel's brother, George, was born. This was a difficult birth for Rose, and she was never very well afterward. George was taken permanently out of grade school when the teacher posted the children's IQ scores on the blackboard. He was perhaps developmentally disabled, but definitely uneducated. Poor chap. I remember him being very sociable, and he loved to dance.

Childhood Traumas

Rachel had a difficult childhood in some respects. Children made fun of her clothing and her excellent literary skills, so she didn't have many friends. In her journal, she wrote:

I am in school, 7 years old. All the children walk on the other side of the street. No one comes near me. They laugh at me, taunt me. I am very lonely. One day when I go to school, the children laugh at me. I have worn my dirty apron to school. I remember this for a long time.

There is a boy in school who is always in trouble. The teacher has him stand up front while we put our heads down on our desks so that we cannot see what the teacher is doing. We hear a loud "swack!" and the boy cries out, goes to his desk and sobs. We look up—teacher is putting a ruler back on her desk. I am very upset inside, feel very sorry for the boy, want to cry too.

One day in school, I had a most pleasant experience. I recited Woodrow Wilson's [1917] speech to the American people in declaring war. In part it said, "For the right is more precious than peace, and we shall fight for the things nearest our hearts, for democracy for the rights of those who submit to autocracy to have a voice in their own government," etc. Everyone clapped and I was so proud! At last, I was a person, at last I had been recognized.

Photo 37: Rose Shepard in a Nurse's Uniform

A Blind Date

Photo 38: Rose Shepard, Age 44, with Rachel, Age 5

Photo 39: Rachel, Age 8, with George, Age 4

All through high school, she was forced to wear high-top lace-up boys' shoes that were two sizes too big, which were meant to last a long time. She was a good student and loved to recite long passages of poetry. I think she must have been very resilient. I know she was curious and mischievous, for she said that she once tried to drown a hen and then still felt guilty about it at age 90. Can you imagine the explosion of wet feathers and sharp claws? Her father was strict and didn't show much warmth. He would often lock her in the barn to keep her from wandering off.

Photo 40: Rachel (far right) at York Beach, Maine, ca. 1926

Off to College

Living in rough-and-tumble mining camps and a politically corrupt San Francisco with over 2,000 saloons probably colored Herman's view of the world. He was a very strait-laced minister, and not in favor of Rachel attending college. But she prevailed by getting a loan from New Hampshire State College, borrowing money from friends, and getting a Grange scholarship, as well as working during the summers at beach resorts, possibly as a house cleaner. At heart, Rachel was a bit of a rebel.

A Blind Date

The money she borrowed was from a family of whom her father did not approve because of business dealings that had gone bad, but those friends were always good to Rachel.

Photo 41: Rachel (sitting behind the child) at York Beach, Maine, ca. 1926

Photo 42: Rachel (2nd from right) at York Beach, Maine, ca. 1926

A Rocky Ride

In a journal entry, she describes taking a motorcycle ride with Tom. While she was sitting in the sidecar, they hit the guy-wire on a power pole, and the sidecar turned over. About that incident, she wrote:

> *Well, I am in bed again after a motorcycle accident which might have been worse but was bad enough. I have suffered more than I ever suffered before. Every movement, every breath means a knife turned in my side. But suffering I could bear if it weren't for missing exams. I feel quite sure that I shall be unable to take them. What a mess! But I can say and say honestly that I am glad of this, it has meant such wonderful peace and joy because of Tom. When I regained consciousness and heard him crying my name with awful sobs, when I saw the fear and pain in his face, it was joy unspeakable to hold him in my arms and kiss him again and again, to have him there safe and only slightly injured. To see how much he cared and when we lay on the side of the hill with his arms around me. Oh! I was so happy just to be with him and love him. My cup runneth over. That Saturday night has made all the difference in the world. I probably shall never marry him, but we can be happy while there is time left. He sent me a box of candy today. He is worried. Oh, how I miss him!*[14]

Photo 43: Rachel, ca. 1920s

---

[14]Rachel E. Shepard, Diary, June 7, 1926, n.p.

A Blind Date

When she returned to her dormitory, Rachel had to climb the stairs on her hands and knees. She ultimately took her final exams from her bed.

The motorcycle, a Harley, was ill-fated. Tom loaned the bike to a friend, who subsequently crashed it through a local U.S. Post Office window. The friend returned the bike to Tom, never saying a word about the accident. After those two incidents, Tom prudently sold the motorcycle. It's no wonder he never wanted my brother, Larry, to have one.

In Rachel's senior year of college, her mother was ailing badly from kidney disease. Rachel offered to go home to take care of her, but her father added strong stipulations about what she would be allowed to do and what she wouldn't. For example, she wouldn't be allowed to date, or to associate with some of her friends, or to attend any church but his. However, her mother begged her to finish college, which she did, knowing that she would be a virtual slave to her father if she stayed. Since her father wanted her to take care of her mother, I don't believe he ever forgave her for going against his wishes. He was a very strict and unbending man, not one for compassion. As a child, mom was scared of him. I never knew my grandfather, which may be just as well. However, he was probably the one who instilled such a strong moral compass in my mother. Although he was a graduate of Harvard University and Andover Theological Seminary, he seemed to disdain people of wealth, according to my mother.

At one time, Rachel had hoped to become a teacher, but after a stint of "practice teaching," in which she found herself with a bunch of unruly children, she returned to finish her bachelor's degree. Teaching was not for her, and marriage would have precluded her career as a teacher in any case. Perhaps that influenced my idea of what teaching involves, since I never wanted to be one. Isn't it interesting that both of my college-educated grandfathers were against college education for their children?

While working at the poultry plant on campus, Tom had many dreams. First and foremost, he wanted to become a writer and enrolled in a correspondence class for screenwriters. He thought perhaps he could team up with his father, who also liked to write. Rachel helped him in those endeavors, as is clear in his lovely letter to her in March of 1927:

> *Dear Rachel,*
>
> *I am alone today and very, very lonesome all because of you, for there is a faint odor of your powder upon a pillow which you used and the kittens also smell very nice in spite of their mother's unappreciativeness, by continued licking and washing of their "furry" little bodies. And so all that I have today is yesterday's happiness, which is truly a lot—but I'm still unsatisfied—I want you, Rachel, more and more. It is seldom that we can be alone together to talk and play as we did yesterday, and it was wonderful. You don't know what a big thrill it gave me to see you washing those dishes, and helping me count those baby chickens. Just helping me. But best of all, how attentive you were in listening to me when I read the outline of my manuscript; how kind and considerate you were of my mistakes in English; and of how much you encouraged me. This all means so much to me; and the realization of the fact that I have someone who loves me and understands my perhaps foolish attempt in creative work, gives me much courage and confidence, and I hope that maybe sometime I may be worthy of you. Few men, Rachel dear, are so lucky to have a girl like you; your education and fine sensibilities ought always to keep me on my toes.*

When Rachel eventually agreed to marry Tom, she extracted a promise from him that he would finish four years of college. It would be a long time before that came to pass, close to twenty years.

An Unexpected Friendship

While Tom was at the University of New Hampshire, he met Ching Foh Bau, a young man from China who was observing the poultry industry, and was born on the very same day as Tom: January 18, 1902. Tom was very likable, interested in other people, and made friends easily. Ching Foh Bau wanted Tom to go back to China with him to manage his huge estates. But since Tom was engaged to Rachel at the time, and also going to school, he turned down the opportunity, as well as a world tour. But he and Ching Foh Bau remained good friends and corresponded over the years. Almost thirty years later, Ching Foh Bau sent both my sister and me wedding gifts from the Philippines, where he relocated after leaving China during World War II.

Photo 44: Ching Foh Bau and Tom, ca. 1927

Graduation, But No Diploma

Rachel, who had majored in French, graduated from the University of New Hampshire in 1927 with a B.A. degree in Liberal Arts. Because of her poor health, her mother was unable to attend, and I presume her father didn't go either.

Photo 45: Rachel in Her Graduation Gown, 1927

Rachel didn't receive her actual diploma until she paid her delinquent college fees, which she did by working at the University Agricultural Experiment Station as a laboratory assistant in poultry husbandry.[15] I don't know what the job entailed, but I expect it was very menial, tedious work. A note from Tom to Rachel's father indicated that it was a terrible situation. However, Rachel was determined to pay off her debts and would not consider marriage until she had done so. When she applied for a job at the New York Public Library, she didn't have enough money to travel for the interview. So, she applied for another library job, this one in Brookline, Massachusetts, but was wearing her engagement ring at the interview, which she later felt probably cost her the position. I assume, however, that Tom was relieved.

Photo 46: Rachel, ca. the Late 1920s

---

[15]Bulletin of the University of New Hampshire: *The University of New Hampshire and New Hampshire College and Mechanic Arts,* vol. 19, no. 5, p. 15 (February 1928), Dover, New Hampshire.

Whoopee! Marriage

Soon after Rachel finished paying her fees, the couple were married on February 5, 1928, in Dover, New Hampshire. Dr. Elton M. Gildow, a veterinarian in the university's Poultry Department at that time, and his wife, Florence, "stood up with them," to use the phrase of the time. The Gildows' wedding gift, a heavy wooden rolling pin, is now proudly owned by my niece, Nancy Hathaway. Rachel's parents did not attend the wedding, and I don't believe they were even invited. Apparently, Tom had not asked Rachel's father for her hand in marriage. Rachel's mom, Rose Etta, would not have been able to attend in any case, due to her failing health. In fact, a few weeks later, on March 15, 1928, she passed away.

Photo 47: Tom on His Wedding Day, February 5, 1928

In an undated letter to Tom, Rachel's father wrote:

> *She married without my approval or disapproval and in fact nearly or quite without my knowledge, and planned her future likewise alone as far as I was concerned or consulted. Had I been consulted and objected, I might have done you and her harm rather than good. Time will tell and of course I hope for the best.*

Seeds of Hope, Fields of Disappointment

As early as 1925, Tom corresponded with his own father about returning to Cassopolis, Michigan. He planned to help his dad and brother, Max, at Rolling Meadows, the Higgins homestead, which had belonged to his grandparents. His grandmother, Caroline Higgins, was still living there and needed help with the farm. Jay P., dad's father, did not want to be a farmer, but he felt obligated to take care of the farm for his mother. His health was not good, so he didn't know if he could hold out much longer.

Tom had many plans for improving the Michigan farm, including adding a large orchard, increasing the poultry production, and beginning market gardening. Over the next couple of years, there were many letters back and forth between Tom and his parents, as well as a contract of sorts. Tom's parents told him that his brother, Max, and Max's wife, Lois, would be moving out once Max found a job. They wanted a place by themselves and were not keen on farming. In addition, Jay P. and Mabel also wanted to find a small place for themselves in town once Tom got things established. That looked like a wonderful opportunity for Tom to return to Michigan to put the farm on a good footing.

I'm not sure that Rachel wanted to become a farmer's wife, but she was eager to help Tom in his efforts. Because she no longer had work obligations, they threw all caution to the wind and set out for Michigan.

Chapter 4:
Michigan to Maine

Tom and Rachel arrived in Michigan around June 1928 to much turmoil and a heavy workload. But it was not *all* work, since Tom found time to join the community band in Cassopolis.

*Photo 48: The Cassopolis Community Band
(Tom is 4th from the left in the back row)*

He wrote to his father-in-law that Rachel was doing remarkably well managing the house, but was somewhat homesick. There were still no modern conveniences and no running water in the house. Tom's work was moving slowly due to rainy weather, but he nevertheless managed to take care of two thousand chickens, five head of cattle, nine acres of field corn, nearly four acres of early and late potatoes, and six acres of very good alfalfa hay. The fact that there were only 19 acres of field crops in use says a lot, since Tom's grandfather, Thomas T., at one time had 200 acres under cultivation. What had caused the decline in arable crops in just a few short years? Were plummeting crop prices the cause, or was it Jay P.'s lack of farming experience or work ethic?

In any case, all was not well. By September, Max had still not found a job, and he, Lois, and their baby, Margaret Ann, were still at the farm. As Rachel recounted to her father:

> Tom and I are contemplating returning East this Fall. A definite date has not yet been decided on. The fact is that altho' Tom has had splendid success with his chickens and crops, he and his parents have disagreed so much that it is useless to stay. His brother and wife are problems. His brother seems unable to hold a job, and he and his family have been living with us the past two weeks. Tom and Max don't get along.

Rachel later wrote in a journal:

> It was a disaster. We stayed [for] six months of agony, constant battling with Tom's dad and his brother. Tom's old grandmother [Caroline] was there, she and I hit it off fairly well, as did Tom's mother and I. His dad didn't approve of my cooking, especially the lettuce salad (rabbit food).

In a letter to Rachel's father, Tom wrote:

> As you know, the folks were to give me full possession here this fall, but as the time drew near for them to do so I could see that they had no intent, never did have any intentions of doing so—they only thought that they might.

It wasn't long before family tensions and rivalries between Tom and his younger brother, Max, escalated, until one day a fight broke out between the brothers. Apparently, Tom threw a punch at Max, but hit his mother instead. Max threatened to call the police. Tom adored his mother, Mabel, as did Rachel. But after this incident, the sheriff suggested that it would be best for them to leave the state. Tom wrote to Rachel's father:

> *We are leaving here on or about the first of December for Eliot, Maine where I shall take over the management of a poultry plant and farm. This position shall have to do until I can better myself. We expect to drive through, and of course we will stop off in West Epping, NH to see you and George.*

Rachel's father responded to Tom in an undated letter:

> *It is easy enough to know quicksand when you see one sinking in it. It is another matter to detect it before stepping on it, and perhaps I knew no better than you or Rachel what awaited you in Michigan. It was only my intuition and many years of contact with all sorts and conditions of people, good and bad, ignorant and brilliant, East and West, that made me at heart really have little faith in the Michigan venture. Had I tried to hold you back, Rachel may have felt, had you and she listened to me, that I had done you and her irreparable injury and spoiled your lives. You and she have tried it and now I trust you are satisfied.*

Oh, my! An I-told-you-so letter. It was a difficult time to find employment, but while Tom was at New Hampshire State College, Mrs. Florence "Kitty" Schopflocher from Eliot, Maine, offered him a job if he ever needed one. How he happened to meet her is a mystery. The job was at the summer home of the wealthy Schopflocher family, a farm called Nine Gables, though none of the buildings had nine gables. Tom and Rachel packed up once again and headed for Maine.

Rachel wrote:

> *We had a charming cottage in a romantic setting. I loved the little apartment, completely furnished with a loggia in Oriental style with large hanging lamps elaborately decorated, oriental rugs and tiger skins. Mrs. Schopflocher promised to build a garage for Tom's car. Kitty [i.e., Mrs. Schopflocher] invited*

us over to her house for Christmas dinner where we were wined and dined in great luxury with the full-length portrait of 'Abdu'l-Bahá, Bahá'í's prophet behind us.[16]

According to Rachel, this where the Bahá'í hoped to build a great university.

Photo 49: Interior of Tom and Rachel's "Old Bull" Cottage, ca. 1955

The Schopflochers and the Bahá'í

Mrs. Schopflocher (1886–1970) was a fascinating, striking woman. She and her husband, Siegfried, a wealthy businessman in Montreal, were active in the Bahá'í community in that city and in Eliot, Maine. They contributed heavily to the organization and traveled extensively. "Kitty"—or "Lorol," as she was also known—traveled around the world nine times, visiting eighty-six countries, where she promoted their religion.[17]

---

[16]Rachel S. Higgins, Journal, ca. 2000.

[17]Florence (Lorol) Schopflocher, *Bahá'í Chronicles: A Journal to the Past and Present*, available at https://bahaichronicles.org/florence-lorol-schopflocher/.

Photo 50: Nine Gables

The Bahá'í faith teaches the essential worth of all religions and the unity of all people. Established by Bahá'u'lláh in the nineteenth century in Persia and parts of the Middle East, it has faced ongoing persecution since its inception. When Bahá'u'lláh's son, 'Abdu'l-Bahá, was asked, "What is a Bahá'í?" he replied: "To be a Bahá'í simply means to love all the world; to love humanity and try to serve it; to work for universal peace and universal brotherhood."[18] I like that concept.

From an article posted to a Bahá'í internet discussion group, R. Jackson Armstrong-Ingram, a Bahá'í scholar, wrote about Lorol:

> *She had a uniquely personal style of "travel teaching." It might be summed up by the comment of one shipboard dance companion that she had the best legs he had ever seen on a missionary. Men found her immensely attractive and she used this blatantly to get her own way.*[19]

---

[18]*Free Bahá'í Faith*, available at https://freebahais.blogspot.com/.

[19]Keith Ransom-Kehler and Lorol Schopflocher, *Notes at Haifa,* May 12, 1932, available at https://www.h-net.org/~bahai/diglib/MSS/P-T/ransom.htm/.

Rachel wrote:

> *Kitty was the owner of several beautiful and rare Saluki dogs given her by the Queen of Romania. She used to ask me to walk them for her. They were very lively and hard to control.*

Tom managed the farm, Nine Gables, while Rachel became a companion to Kitty, with whom she was quite taken, as she learned many of the social niceties of entertaining the upper class. Kitty's friend, Ivy Edwards, a pleasant lady, also took a liking to Rachel and asked her to visit with her in Kitty's beautifully decorated colonial style house. Ivy tried to interest Rachel in the Bahá'í faith, gave her some literature about it and also some very pretty Fiestaware dishes. That's an interesting tidbit, since we grew up using Fiestaware dishes in our home. I had no idea that the initial pieces came from Tom and Rachel's short stay in Maine.

Jealous Chauffeur

Kitty and her chauffeur, Lionel Loveday, appeared to have a very close relationship. He took her to Boston for medical treatment once a week, apparently for a tarantula bite. My parents didn't quite believe the subterfuge, and feelings between the chauffeur and Tom were tense. Lionel carried a knife, which he flourished now and then, and was obviously jealous of Tom. Perhaps he felt that Tom spent too much time with Kitty. Or maybe the fact that Tom and Rachel were given a lovely cottage to live in and were invited guests in Kitty's home was galling to Lionel.

My parents didn't stay very long in Maine. Siegfried, Kitty's husband, was away on business much of the time, so Kitty was lonely. As Rachel recounted, Kitty treated her and Tom very well. As I mentioned before, Kitty was an attractive woman, and also a flirt. Lionel, the chauffeur, saw Kitty crying on Tom's shoulder one day and went after him with the switchblade knife. Tom was a handsome young man, so Lionel apparently made assumptions about that. I would have thought that Lionel would have been fired, but he wasn't, so Tom and Rachel decided that it was time to leave. Thus, another chapter in their first year of marriage had ended. However, I do know that Tom was looking elsewhere for a job anyway, and perhaps he felt confident that he would find something.

Photo 51: Lorol Schopflocher, ca. 1920s

Chapter 5:
On to Rhode Island

In somewhat less than a year, Tom and Rachel moved once again, but this time with no job in sight. Their lifeline was the Pearson family in New Hampshire, where Tom had lived and worked prior to attending New Hampshire State College. The Pearsons graciously allowed them to stay with them until Tom could find a job. Fortunately, in April 1929, just before the Great Depression, Tom found a job managing Sunny Ridge Farm in Kingston, Rhode Island, which was owned by M. H. Brightman, a former Assistant Professor of Poultry Husbandry. When he hired Tom, however, he was the Chief of the Bureau of Markets at the Rhode Island State Department of Agriculture. Mr. Brightman described the potential job for Tom in a letter he wrote to him in March 1929:

> *I have a capacity for 1500 layers and have brooders for 5000 chicks. We are carrying mostly Leghorns at the present time, together with a few Rocks; however, I am getting into the Red game this Spring.[20] I will pay $100.00 a month, furnish the house, light, telephone, water, eggs and chickens to the desirable party. We have a good going poultry business and the right man who is willing to show sufficient interest can make a very good thing of it. The house has all modern conveniences and is located in a very fine community.*

Kingston had once been prosperous, but was in decline commercially due to locally thriving mill towns nearby. It was a small sleepy village in 1929, with a growing college presence. Rhode Island College of Agriculture and Mechanical Arts had been founded there in 1890, and

---

[20]Leghorns, Barred Rocks, Plymouth Rocks, and Rhode Island Reds are all common varieties of chickens.

changed its name to Rhode Island State College in 1909. By 1929, it had 93 graduates, and there were less than 500 residents in town, many of whom worked at the college. Formerly called Little Rest, Kingston now included a country store, a library, a post office, a grammar school, and a Congregational church. The main street had many fine old historic buildings, and still does to this day.

Photo 52: The Main Street of Kingston As It Is Today
(The building in the foreground is the former post office)

In a letter to Rachel's father on April 23, 1929, Tom wrote:

> *You perhaps have wondered how we like it here and how we are getting along. We like it fine. We have a nice place to live with all the modern conveniences. My employers are very nice to us. Mr. Brightman and his wife have put themselves out needlessly in many instances to make us comfortable. The farm that we are located on is on the Kingston ridge up high and dry. It is very beautiful country. There are but few pines around here. The timber is mostly oak with a sprinkling of maple and elm.*
> *The people of the community are of a somewhat higher*

caliber because Kingston is a college town. There is quite a bit of broken-down aristocracy—dead broke. Kingston was at one time the capital of the state. This section is very rich in Indian lore and history. At one time there were many slaves as there were no small farms—all large plantations.

Some of this history is new to me. I was aware that Kingston had been the capital of Rhode Island, and in fact it was one of five rotating state capitals between 1776 and 1791. I didn't know there were large plantations in the area with slaves. In school, we were only taught about the slavery in the South. I concluded at that time that there were no slaves in the North. How little I knew.

Photo 53: A Plaque Showing the Original Name of Kingston

Continuing his letter to Rachel's father, Tom wrote:

> *Mr. Smith, who is Mr. Brightman's partner, is manager and part owner of the Flint-Adaskin furniture store of Providence. He gave us about a 30% reduction on all of our purchases. We found, however, that to buy a bed such as the one we have and a chest of drawers that it would be pretty expensive. We have been wondering if you could send it to us? I hate to ask this favor of you because I know that you are busy. All expenses of getting it ready and sent down here by freight I shall be more than willing to pay. I can send a crate up for the bedstead if you could give me the height and width. The mattress and springs would not have to be crated, as I sent them on from Michigan uncrated. There is no rush. Anytime during the next ten or fourteen days will be time enough, and there ought to be plenty of rainy days.*

This all seems quite bizarre to me, but times are very different now. People don't squeeze their pennies as hard as they did when I was young. Tom never bought cheaply made furniture, so if his bed and chest were good quality, it would make sense to ship them. He expected furniture to last a lifetime. Freight charges must have been very low to make the effort worthwhile. It's hard to imagine the mattress and springs being sent uncrated. I'm not sure I would have wanted a mattress of mine traveling that way. But it must have been difficult for Tom to ask his father-in-law to send the furniture, since their relationship seems to have been fraught with tension. After all, Tom had married Rachel without her father's approval. Herman had been skeptical of them going to Michigan and then to Maine, and now here they were in Rhode Island.

In September 1929, after their first summer in Kingston, Rachel wrote to her father:

> *We like it here very much and have enjoyed the summer. Our garden has done exceptionally well even tho' Tom didn't have time to give it much care. Mr. Brightman informed Tom this morning that he was giving him $120 [per year] raise. Not so bad after six months, is it? I am quite busy now canning tomatoes, making jelly and pickles. Write when you can find time.*

Photo 54: Rachel at Sunny Ridge Farm, ca. 1929

Photo 55: Rachel in a Car at Sunny Ridge Farm, ca. 1929

In a journal dated 1990, when she was 84 years old, Rachel wrote about Sunny Ridge Farm:

> *We enjoyed it there, privacy, many farm animals, I made my own butter, we had eggs and vegetables from the farm and we were able to save money.*

Tom was lucky to have a job during the depression era, but life was even harder for his family in Michigan. In a letter to my sister, Teresa, in September of 1978, he wrote:

> *The times were desperate in the 1930s. In 1929 or '30 my folks were so behind in taxes, Federal Land Bank payments, etc. that we sent them all the money we had. It saved the farm.*

I suspect that would have been a couple of hundred dollars at most, but that was a large sum in 1930. Tom was never repaid any of it, but that was fine with him.

In another letter to Teresa, Tom wrote that times were equally rough for Uncle Claude, Jay P.'s brother. But Claude's fun was good medicine, as we see in the letter:

> *When Uncle Claude Higgins visited [when Tom was a boy], he never lost time getting into his funny stories and acts to hear mother laugh. He was a terrific mimic. When Larry [as a boy] mimics, it reminds me of Uncle Claude. He had some acts you would never forget. One of an old farmer who limped with a cane, hard of hearing and stuttered. The act had many variations; one: his favorite bloodhound got loose when in heat and went courting down the road to another farm, the farmer being no friend. Uncle Claude being a good ventriloquist would then put on the act—the crippled farmer, the neighbor farmer and the two dogs. He would put on an imaginary exit and entrance limping with the cane, his glasses pulled down on his nose, looking cross-eyed, his suspenders unbuttoned in back so that his pants looked like they were about to fall off. So close in proximity of the stove and wood box these imaginary characters faced each other over the dogs. They proceeded to insult each other—the stuttering and stammering increasing with the old man who then dramatically paused and stuffed*

> *his mouth with imaginary chewing tobacco and proceeded with the argument only pausing to spit imaginary gobs on the wood in the wood box. Uncle Claude never failed with his audience. His mimicking of local politicians in an argument was hilarious.*

I can just imagine Dad, with his face red and taut with repressed mirth as he was writing this to my sister.

The story that Dad claimed had left the biggest impression on him as a youngster was one about the former owner of the neighboring Williams' farm. As Dad related in a letter to a cousin of his:

> *The farmer had witnessed a balloonist parachute out of a hot-air balloon at the county fair and figured he could do something similar. Using the big wagon umbrella, he climbed to the peak of the barn roof and jumped off. It had rained recently and was soggy below. Falling faster than he expected, he found a very soft landing in straw and cow manure up to his elbows. The man was a bedraggled sight, and stuttered and stammered almost uncontrollably. His wife couldn't understand him but made him take a bath in the old wash tub under the apple trees before she would let him in the house. Uncle Claude made the most of the stuttering and stammering as he fine-tuned the story.*

What a hilarious tale for a young boy to hear.

Mabel, Dad's mother, adored Uncle Claude and his humor. It was a huge loss to her when he died in 1929 at age 51. Here's an odd thing: Dad mentions my brother Larry mimicking someone, but neither my sister nor I remember Larry mimicking anyone, unless it was when he was teasing us. And my brother now says that he never mimics anyone intentionally.

Chapter 6:
East Farm

The 1930s

What a dramatic first year of marriage my parents had. Five moves and on to their sixth. I expect they thought they had hit the jackpot when, in May of 1930, a new job opened at East Farm that required a manager. The salary was $2,200 a year. Little did they know that this would be their last move for many years.

Photo 56: East Farm, ca. 1931
(The Egg-Laying Contest buildings are in the foreground. In the background are the farmhouse (behind the cars), and the barnlike office building is to the right of it)

East Farm, formerly known as the Gough Farm, was a new acquisition by Rhode Island State College in Kingston and was purchased for orchard and poultry research. Its nine acres were located on the east side of Route 108. The college also purchased adjacent land to the east of the property.[21] Tom applied for the job and was hired by Dr. Basil E. Gilbert, Director of the Agricultural Experiment Station at the college.[22] He became manager of the Experimental Poultry Plant and later the supervisor of the Rhode Island Egg-Laying Contest, and remained in the latter capacity along with added job requirements until 1947.

Photo 57: The Sign at the Entrance to East Farm, 2024

---

[21] Dr. Wayne K. Durfee, *University of Rhode Island—East Farm—Poultry, 1947–1970*. University of Rhode Island, May 10, 2003.

[22] Thomas C. Higgins to Dr. Basil E. Gilbert, Letter, May 20, 1930.

Poultrymen from near and far brought chickens to East Farm, and careful records were kept of their egg production for fifty weeks. The purpose of the contest was to stimulate interest in developing a better egg-laying bird. Dr. Wayne Durfee, Professor Emeritus at the University of Rhode Island, provided the following information about the time he worked as a student at the Egg-Laying Contest site:

> *Like Consumer Reports today, Egg Contest reports enabled comparative evaluations of livability and annual egg-laying performance of the breeds, varieties, and strains of birds available from poultry breeders who used the contest reports to promote their available stocks. The Egg-Laying Contest consisted of two long buildings, each of which contained 25 8'x10' pens arranged side-by-side and housed 13 hens each. Each pen was accessed from a walkway that ran along the south side of each row of pens (there were no doors between the pens). The contest year ran from October 1 through August 31. Trap fronts on the nests confined the bird which entered until the attendant released her and identified her egg with her leg band number. At the Head House, each egg was weighed and assigned a point value, related to its size. The Egg-Laying Contests in the 1920s–1950s era were very important in the high egg production birds of today. Two-hundred seventy eggs per bird per year was common.[23]*

The Contest was in operation for well over thirty years.

Photo 58: The Egg-Laying Contest Building, ca. 1950

---

[23]Dr. Wayne K. Durfee to Teresa R. Hathaway, Letter, December 4, 2010.

The old Gough farmhouse at East Farm, which was built in the late 1800s, became Mom and Dad's home, with the rent and utilities free, in exchange for Dad keeping an eye on the farm. During the summers, that included shutting the doors at night on the chicken coops of the young free-range chickens. Once they were about six months old, or of egg-laying age, they were moved into permanent poultry buildings.

Photo 59: The Gough Farmhouse with Nancy Standing in Front, ca. 2020
(It looked much the same when she was a girl)

Photo 60: The Gough Farmhouse as Seen from the Back, 2024

*Photo 61: The Poultry Department Office Building, 2024
(which is now used by the East FarmTrout Research Facility)*

Dad and Mom became active in the community. Between 1929 and 1931, they participated in staged readings of plays by the Kingston Players in Edwards Hall at the college: *Pomeroy's Past*, a three-act comedy, and *So's Your Old Antique*, both by Clare Kummer, to name two. My parents were in the cast of *Pomeroy's Past*, and Dad was the stage manager for at least one of the other plays.[24]

I would have loved to see those performances, since Mom could be very dramatic when she read a poem. I took a series of snapshots of her reciting a poem when she was 99. I have to admit that, before her recitation, she looked like an old crone seated in her recliner, with her teeth on the table beside her and a soiled bib around her neck. But when she was reciting the poem, which she had probably learned as a child, it was magical. Her emotions changed from a benign look to fear, as her eyes flashed in anger, and then to joy and contentment as she ended with a look of mischievousness and a twinkle in her beautiful blue eyes.

---

[24]David Belasco, The Kingston Players Present *The Return of Peter Grimm*, ca. 1931.

I have no memory of the poem, only the emotions on her face, which I cherish.

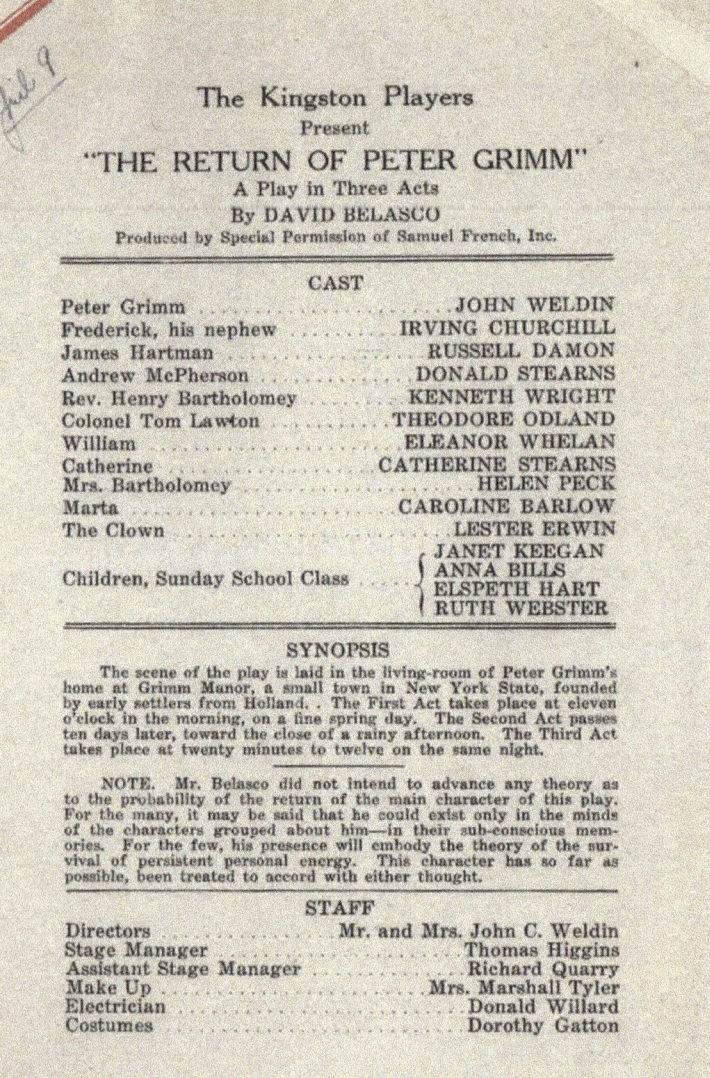

Photo 62: Playbill for "The Return of Peter Grimm," Presented by the Kingston Players

A highlight of her early years in Kingston was an invitation in 1932 to join the Every Tuesday Club, which had been founded in 1896 and functioned as a small literary group for women. Many of the members were from Kingston, and in the early years membership was limited to fifteen. Most of the members were wives of professors and administrators at the Rhode Island State College (later the University of Rhode Island), local clergy, and other prominent men in town.

Mom was 26 and pregnant with my brother at the time, so she initially declined to join, writing to the club:

> *After thinking it over, I have decided that I do not feel it wise for me to become a member of the Tuesday Club at present because of the expense and the probable difficulty in getting someone to stay with the baby when it arrives.*[25]

Photo 63: Larry at 1 Year Old

---

[25]Rachel S. Higgins to Miss Isabel Eddy, Letter, May 4, 1932, *Every Tuesday Club Collection*, Minutes, Files, Yearbooks, 1876-2003. South County History Center, Kingston, Rhode Island.

Somehow, her circumstances changed and she was listed as a member, starting in 1933. The invitation was a huge thrill for her, since it meant that she was accepted into the community. Dad at the time was an uneducated farm manager, but Mom had a college degree, which I suspect most of the other women did not. Members of the club shared book reviews and papers on history, literature, and the culture of foreign countries, in meetings that they held at members' homes, including ours.[26] Mom speculated in later years that perhaps her calling cards or her college education had made an impression on the members. Calling cards or visiting cards were used in the nineteenth and early twentieth centuries, so Mom, being ever so proper, etiquette wise, definitely used them.

My parents' first child, Lawrence, was born in 1932, followed by identical twin sisters, Teresa and me, in 1935.

Photo 64: Mom and Larry at the Beach, ca. 1933

---

[26]*Every Tuesday Club Collection*, Minutes, Files, Yearbooks, 1876-2003. South County History Center, Kingston, Rhode Island.

Photo 65: Mom and Dad at Christmastime, ca.1942

Poor Mom! She hadn't expected twins. When I was 70 or so, she told me how she had turned her head to the wall and cried when the doctor told her she had twins.

I laughed and said, "Tough luck, Mom!"

Then she went on to say that she became incensed when the doctor offered to find another home for one of us—probably me.

I'm not sure Mom was enamored of having a family, since she really would have liked to work in some capacity and be respected for her intelligence. However, at that time, most married women did not work outside the home, and Dad certainly would not have approved. In an undated journal entry, Mom wrote, "Children were more a burden than a joy."

That was a bit unsettling to read and was most likely during our early years. I think Larry was very active and a challenge, whereas we twins were content with amusing ourselves. But perhaps we were a challenge, too.

Photo 66: Larry, Age 4, in Front of a Chicken Coop

Photo 67: Dad, Larry, Mom, and the Twins, ca. 1937

Photo 68: Larry and the Twins, ca. 1938

Photo 69: Teresa and Nancy in Jammies, 1938

Photo 70: Larry Wearing a Suit that Dad Had Made for Him

East Farm

Photo 71: Nancy, Larry, Mom, and Teresa (in front of Great-Grandpa Shepard's Farmhouse, West Epping, New Hampshire, ca. 1939)

Dad continued to play his trumpet in a community orchestra and dabbled with art projects, which included several batiks, one of which I have today. In fact, it may be my favorite piece of his. Sadly, his other batiks have disappeared.

Dad painted a self-portrait, using pastels, and also tried woodcarving. I have a wooden tray with handles carved in the shape of nudes (Photo 75). He created most of his art prior to the arrival of his children or when we were very young. He made a plaster cast of Larry's head, which must have been a very unpleasant experience for Larry. I'm sure I would find it claustrophobic to be covered by plaster-coated strips of cloth.

Photo 72: One of Dad's Batiks, Probably Dating from the Late 1930s

Photo 73: Self-Portrait of Dad, ca. 1930s

I doubt that Dad had any art instruction as a child, but his work showed considerable talent. In a newspaper article, he is quoted as saying:

My interest in art has been almost lifelong. As a youngster, I had a lot of fun with watercolors. My materials were limited to rolls of leftover wallpaper. I would spend hours upstairs. When the Titanic sank in that iceberg collision, I had no idea of the enormity of the situation, but I did sink the Titanic many times on wallpaper.[27]

Photo 74: Plaster Cast of Larry's Head, ca. 1938

---

[27]Arnold W. Peterson, "Tom Higgins, a 20th-Century Renaissance Man," *Narragansett Times*, September 28, 1990, pp. 3A and 10A.

Photo 75: Wooden Tray with Nude Handles, ca.1940s

In later years, Dad often wrote about his family:

> *My folks like most everybody out there were terribly poor. No Jobs—farm prices at rock bottom. Nobody ate very well. In one of mother's letters, eggs were 20 cents a dozen and wheat was 35 cents a bushel. Later corn even got to 65 cents a bushel. In 1937 the Higgins farm grossed nearly $700.00. That's affluence for you!*

I think Dad was being a bit facetious here, since $700.00 in 1937 would only be $12,662 in today's dollars. And that was a gross figure, before expenses were deducted. Remember, his parents were trying to make a living by selling farm products.

In the 1930s, Mabel, Dad's mom, came down with Hodgkin's disease, which is cancer of the lymph nodes. The x-ray treatments made her deathly ill, and she simply wasted away. Dad wrote:

> *She fought hard to live, even in her letters. She maintained a steady courage, no self-pity. Everybody loved mother.*

Mabel died in 1937 at the age of 55. Dad said that we twins always reminded him of his mother.

In the late 1930s, Dad was still painting in his spare time. One 1936 pastel in particular came to the attention of Dr. John Weldin, a professor of bacteriology at the college where Dad worked. It was a copy of the cover of the *Literary Digest* from October 20, 1928, which portrayed a woman holding a bowl of fruit. The original painting by Julius Ralshoven, an American artist, was entitled "The Vintage," and hung in the Grand Central Art Galleries in New York City. Dr. Weldin was so impressed by Dad's rendition that he described it to the president of the college, Dr. Bressler, who, when he saw the pastel, encouraged Dad to return to school to finish his bachelor's degree.

Photo 76: "The Vintage" by Julius Ralshoven

Photo 77: Dad's 12.5" x 18" Copy of "The Vintage," ca. 1936

With the support of those gentlemen, Dad eventually returned to college on a part-time basis. Apparently, his previous classes at Michigan State University and the University of New Hampshire counted for little when he started school again. Too many years had passed, and requirements had changed. According to Larry, Dad first studied a very fat book called *High School Self-Taught* in order to obtain the equivalent of a GED. That was news to me. I imagine it was difficult for him to attend classes while having a full-time job, but his bosses must have made accommodations for him.

In the late 1930s, the Works Progress Administration (WPA) had workers at East Farm blasting tree stumps to clear land for peach and apple orchards. Larry wrote the following about that:

> *Unbelievably, there was a significant stash of dynamite in the building less than 300 ft. from our home. I explored this thoroughly, including the blasting caps and the plunger dynamo that detonated them. I thought about electrically igniting a dynamite cap but chickened out, thankfully. I just looked around! When the WPA was working on the farm, they let me jam the plunger down to blow the tree stumps. They were blown near our house, which often was pelted with roots and dirt from the explosions. I also learned to drive a Caterpillar tractor while sitting between the knees of Ed, a black WPA worker.*

I remember the house being pelted, and I think my sister and I were told to stay inside. I really wanted to go out to see the action. The dynamite that Larry found was probably for general farm use and for the WPA people to use, which was not an uncommon occurrence on farms where land was being cleared. That was the horticultural side of farm operations, so Dad was not involved. However, the WPA workers also built at least one long wooden poultry building and some of the larger granite buildings on the main campus, including classrooms and the library. A few years later, Teresa and I found a bunker deep in the far end of the farm that contained explosives. Maybe that was the final storage place for no longer needed dynamite. After we talked about our discovery, the bunker soon acquired a locked door.

The Early 1940s

While playing with matches one day, Teresa and I inadvertently set the barn on fire! We had just turned 6 the day before, so there were probably matches around after we had our birthday cake. Fortunately, it was a very small fire and was quickly put out. We both skedaddled in different directions. I'm not sure where I hid, but as I ran, I saw one of the farmhands rushing in to put out the flames. The volunteer fire department showed up, too. It could have been a disaster, since the barn was filled with bales of wood shavings used for bedding in chicken coops. The story was reported in *The Providence Journal*, but our names were left out. The headline was: "Children with Matches Blamed for Fire at State College Farm."[28] Since we were the only children at the farm, it was pretty obvious who the culprits were. The story read:

> *A fire believed to have been started by children playing with matches ignited approximately 60 bales of shavings in the poultry building at East Farm of R.I. State College on Kingstown Road, Kingston, yesterday afternoon.*
>
> *The blaze was among a number of grass and brush fires which kept South Kingstown and Narragansett fire departments busy yesterday. While the Kingston Volunteer Fire Department was extinguishing the East Farm blaze, another alarm for a grass fire in the rear of the Washington County Jail House at Kingston was sounded.*
>
> *Apparatus from the Union fire district of South Kingstown responded. The college poultry building was undamaged as the Kingston firemen confined the flames in the shavings.*

Although the story claimed that 60 bales of shavings had ignited, I seriously doubt it, for that would have meant that the barn, which was undamaged, had gone up in flames. Perhaps the bales were just singed. My sister got an immediate spanking, but I didn't. I think maybe I had a better hiding place. Teresa speculates that Dad decided she was the instigator, since I tended to be the timid twin. She was furious with Dad that I didn't get a spanking, too. Neither of us had ever been spanked— and never were again. I know I stayed away from Teresa for a couple of days because she was so grumpy. We think Dad felt guilty afterwards, because he never said anything about it again. Now, here's the funny thing about twins—at least the two of us. Teresa thinks *she* started the fire, and I think *I* did. I guess we share the guilt equally. And that's how our memories often work.

---

[28]*The Providence Journal*, Tuesday, April 1, 1941, p. 2.

*Photo 78: East Farm Poultry Department Staff, ca. 1940
(Left to right, standing in front of the Poultry Department office building: unidentified farmhand, Ray Taylor, Stanley Smith, Dr. John Delaplane, Prudy Robinson, Homer Stuart, Tom Higgins, and two other unidentified farmhands)*

Photo 79: Dr. John Weldin and Dad Examining Chickens, ca. 1940

East Farm

Photo 80: One of the Former Poultry Buildings on East Farm, 2024

*Photo 81: Green Hall, Which Housed the College Library
and Administrative Offices, 1939*

On weekends, we often took family drives on Sunday afternoons. At that time, Rhode Island had a fairly dense population around the Providence area, but the rest of the tiny state was still very rural. We lived thirty miles from Providence, which we would visit once or twice a year on shopping trips. I remember that we usually bought boys' jeans, which were six inches too long, so Teresa and I would have to roll up the cuffs until we grew into them (see Photo 101).

The Sunday trips were very special excursions. We would drive down all sorts of winding back roads through wooded areas, past many farms and a little village now and then. Or we might take a coastal route to see the ocean. Occasionally, we would be rewarded with an ice cream cone at the end of the ride.

But one day in particular was a disaster. That was the day that my sister, who was about 5 at the time, fell out of the car as we were driving home. As she explains it:

> *I remember wondering what would happen if I opened the door a little. Then a swoosh and I must have been knocked unconscious. I don't remember any bruises.*

Curiosity almost killed the cat. But luckily for Teresa, Dad was not driving at today's speeds, only about 35 miles per hour, and there was very little traffic. She probably landed on dirt or grass, rather than pavement. I recall Larry and me begging Dad to stop, since he didn't realize what had happened. The doors on our 1937 Plymouth were called suicide doors because of that problem. They were hinged at the back, so if you opened one while the car was moving, it would swing wide open. It didn't take Dad long to turn the handles around on the back doors, so that one had to lift up rather than push down to open them. He thought it was an accident. Little did he know that Teresa had tempted fate on that day.

It must have been around that time, perhaps a little earlier, that the curiosity bug hit me, too. My only memory of that is the mischievous feeling I had of wondering if a drinking glass would go through the wringer of our washing machine. The wringer on an old-style washing machine consisted of two rotating rubber rollers about fourteen inches long. Mom would feed the clothes between the rollers to squeeze out the water. Well, the glass went through alright, but *not* in one piece. The wringer pulled my arm all the way up past my elbow, crushing the glass in my hand. It must have been a bloody mess, but I only have scars on my palm and elbow as evidence. Maybe we were double trouble at times.

Dad made our house comfortable and, in the late 1930s or early 1940s, built an addition onto the living room, which more than doubled the size of that miniscule space. One wall had bookshelves from floor to ceiling that held grandfather Shepard's library—everything from Darwin's *Origin of Species* to Homer's *Iliad* in Greek, as well as complete sets of Shakespeare and Dickens. I now have many of those books on my own shelves. Most of them are replacements purchased by my grandfather for the ones he lost in the 1893 fire in Black Diamond, Washington, where he was a minister.

Our house had two stories, with one bedroom on the first floor and two bedrooms upstairs for the children. The dining room was the oddest one in the house. Although it was very small, it had six doors—which included the front door of the house, as well as doors to the kitchen, the bathroom, the living room, the downstairs bedroom, and the staircase upstairs. And, yes, there was only one bathroom in the house.

Dad always had a camera. I think he used it mostly for work, but also at other times for artistic exercises. I hesitate to mention one photograph he took of my sister and me, stretched out on a couch facing each other—*naked!* I suppose we were around 7, and I recall feeling a bit uncomfortable about it at the time. Now, if I look at it dispassionately, the picture strikes me as artistic. But what was he thinking? It would be inappropriate today.

When we were little children, Dad tried to teach Mom how to drive, but soon threw up his hands in despair. Instead, she learned from Frank Robinson, a Rhode Island State Trooper and the husband of Prudy Robinson, a secretary in Dad's office. Driving gave Mom the freedom to participate in many church activities. She also enjoyed social action projects and was very active in developing the first Head Start program in the area. Later, she became a charter member of the League of Women Voters.

The one downside of all those committee meetings was that Mom was frequently talking on the phone about committee work when we came home from school and wanted her attention. From those experiences, I learned to hate even the thought of committee meetings. In fact, the idea of joining a committee is anathema to me to this day, as it is for my sister.

Mom took a nap almost every day of her life, which at the time I couldn't see the need for. However, in hindsight, that may be why she lived to just a few weeks shy of her hundredth birthday, which would have been on April 14, 2006. We had been planning a party for her and actually gave her one posthumously.

As young children, we had a playhouse in the backyard that had a Dutch door, which was a novelty to me. It reminded me of a door in a fairy tale I had read. I don't remember the arrival of that playhouse, but Larry shared the following:

> *When I was in grade school, Dad arranged for a small shack to be towed to the backyard at East Farm. This became my hobby center, wherein I spent much time. He divided the floor in half—I think the larger portion was for you and Teresa. He helped me string electricity to the shack. I had my chemistry set and electrical stuff there.*

In the 1940s, children's toys were far more limited than they are today. There were Erector Sets, Lincoln Logs, and chemistry sets. I was envious of Larry's Erector Set when Teresa and I were given Lincoln Logs. Working with strips of metal and nuts and bolts seemed much more enjoyable than putting together pieces of wood shaped like logs.

As for the chemistry sets, they included a variety of chemicals for performing scientific experiments. I don't believe that was particularly a girl activity at the time, but it appealed to my sister and me. One day, when Larry was only 9 or 10, he was mixing chemicals on the floor in the kitchen when he burned a hole right through a metal pie plate and the linoleum into the floorboards. Apparently, he had created some combination of metal powder and metal oxide to make thermite. I can't imagine that a child's chemistry set would have the chemicals needed for that, since thermite is a pyrotechnic composition that can create brief bursts of heat and is used for welding metals together and to make incendiary bombs! When I recently asked Larry if the chemicals were included in the chemistry set, he texted back:

> *At this point, I cannot be sure. But the ingredients are commonplace.*
>
> *But there is more to the story: We college brats had access to the R.I.S.C. Chemistry Dept. stockroom. We were allowed to purchase tiny quantities (teaspoonfuls) of chemicals to augment our Porter Chemistry sets. The thermite formula was from a booklet purchased someplace else, most likely via a Popular Mechanics.*

Maybe that is why Dad decided that he needed to find some space where Larry could experiment, and hence the playhouse. Neither my sister nor I remember using the playhouse very much, especially when Larry was in there. Three's a crowd—and after all, he was three years older. Big brothers can be such an annoyance! But after he no longer used the playhouse, I recall playing with my chemistry set in there.

Larry was involved in many activities while he was still a student at Kingston Hill Grammar School. He was a member of the junior branch of the National Aeronautics Society, which led him, under the guidance of Dr. Nicholas Alexander, a professor of aeronautics at the college, to build a scale model of a monastery chapel that was later constructed in Jordanville, New York. Working from blueprints, Larry scaled the dimensions down to three-eighths of an inch per foot. The model was almost a yard long. In his spare time, he worked in the aeronautics lab on the top floor of Ranger Hall at the college, taking over 300 hours to complete the project. One of the practical benefits of building a model was uncovering some structural details that needed revision.[29]

---

[29]Herbert M. Hofford, "The Boy Who Built a Church," *Providence Journal*, October 6, 1946, p. 22.

Photo 82: Larry's Model of Holy Trinity Monastery, 1947[30]
(From the Holy Trinity Monastery and Seminary Photo Collection)

Photo 83: Holy Trinity Monastery, Jordanville, New York, 1948[31]

---

[30] Available at https://nyheritage.contentdm.oclc.org/digital/collection/holytrin01/id/317/rec/87/.

[31] Available at https://nyheritage.contentdm.oclc.org/digital/collection/holytrin01/id/317/rec/87/.

Dad helped Larry build a photo enlarger from an old camera and a light bulb, which Larry used to make many 5" x 7" enlargements. He was also a whiz at fixing radios and electrical devices. At the age of 12, he had a summer job in Billy Main's jewelry shop in Wakefield, to which he had to ride his bike every day, a distance of three miles. The store sold records and radio/record players along with fine watches. Larry worked for radio tech Bob Warner in the back of the store.

World War II

When Pearl Harbor was attacked, according to Larry, Dad rushed out of his office, panicked that he would be drafted and have to go to war. He was 39 at the time. But after a change of heart, he tried to join the Naval Reserve as an officer. However, after failing to gain entry, perhaps because of his age, his family status, and the fact that his job was considered essential, he became a volunteer Air Raid Warden, complete with white helmet and nightstick. His duties included watching for enemy planes from the wooden observation tower that had been built by the Civilian Conservation Corps in 1938. It was located about four miles from our home, at the intersection of Route 1 and Route 138, and is now called the Hannah Robinson Tower. As a cautionary measure, the top of the car's headlights were painted black, and I remember hanging blankets over our windows at night to block the light from enemy planes.

For Mom, that was a difficult time ethically. In 1942, she attended the American Christian Ashram at Lake Winnipesaukee, New Hampshire, where she studied the ideas of pacifism, especially the teachings of Mahatma Gandhi. I suppose you could call her a student of religion, since she studied so many of them. She had a very strong sense of right and wrong, a strong moral compass. At heart, she believed in nonviolence, and participated in the Fellowship of Reconciliation Program and later in anti-nuclear activities. But during the war, she did her part by collecting scrap metal for the war effort and collecting bacon grease and other fats that were used for making war munitions.

Mom was totally opposed to President Roosevelt's Japanese relocation policies. In Kingston, there was a young student of Japanese descent, Harry Endo, who was attending the accelerated ROTC and baccalaureate program at Rhode Island State College. When his family members who lived in California and Colorado were being placed in detention camps, Harry arranged for his younger sister, Mary, to come to Kingston to live with friends, the Schlenkers, and attend the local high school. Mom frequently welcomed both Mary and Harry into our house. Occasionally, Mary became our babysitter, although I have no memory of that—or of any other babysitters, for that matter. Her stay was not without controversy.

Photo 84: An Ad During World War II[32]

---

[32]"*FATS FOR VICTORY*," *The Narragansett Times*, October 27, 1944, p. 3.

Photo 85: Mary Endo and Her Brothers, ca. 1950s

An editorial in *The Narragansett Times* suggested that Japanese-American students should not be put in leadership positions. The article, entitled "Secret Weapon," began as follows:

> *For decades Japan has had a secret weapon—the snivelling smile which masked her barbaric soul....*
> *That ingratiated smile, though, was only a sheath—a smile of Judas which the world has acknowledged since Hirohito's betrayal at Pearl Harbor.*
> *There are thousands of Japanese-Americans in this country. Some of them may be well-disposed to our way of life, to our concept of government. Yet in our treatment of these Japanese-Americans, we should not forget the treacherous secret weapon—that smile of guile—and keep them in their proper place, one of tolerant, yet firm servitude.*
> *The younger generation of Japanese-Americans must learn what we mean by Americanism without the prefix term. They may be in our schools, attending classes and joining in activities, with our own children. But they should not be allowed positions of leadership in our high school clubs, for instance. Such generosity merely continues the Japanese myth of their racial superiority and divinity."*[33]

---

[33]"Secret Weapon," *The Narragansett Times*, March 2, 1945, p. 2.

It's not a stretch to think that this editorial was written because Mary Endo had recently been made President of the Spanish Club at South Kingstown High School.[34] The editorial inspired the local priest, Father James Greenan, to write a scathing letter that denounced individuals who were criticizing American citizens. I remember Mom being quite incensed over the issue and wholeheartedly supporting Father Greenan. After his letter appeared, negative comments in the paper ceased.

My father disapproved of Mom working outside the home, a typical male response in those days. He even forbade her to babysit. However, she was a very active volunteer over the years. She helped to found a community daycare center that enabled young parents to continue their education, and she was an active member for many years of the Kingston Congregational Church.[35] Her pacifism extended to family interactions. I can't recall her *ever* becoming angry or cross. She always had a smile on her face and a quick wit. When she was in her nineties, I asked her about that, and she said her mother had taught her that it was important to always keep a happy face. Mom was playful at times with words. One of her favorite phrases when she wanted Teresa or me to get her something was, "Would you be so kind and condescending, stoop so low and be so bending as to get me my...." It could be a book, a pencil, or a cup of tea, but whatever it was, I was always amused.

Although I was only 6 when the Japanese bombed Pearl Harbor, I remember seeing patriotic propaganda messages everywhere—in the schools, in newspapers and magazines, at movie theatres, as well as in posters in public places. There were campaigns to save metal and grease, to buy savings bonds, and to grow Victory Gardens. Larry wrote about our Victory Garden:

> *We had a large garden during the war. I helped hoe and rake and picked big old tomato hornworms off the plants. Dad and I worked together. I learned to use a hand cultivator and create "hills" for the corn.*

---

[34]"Activities Clubs Revived at South," *The Narragansett Times*, October 27, 1944, p. 3.

[35]Bob McCreanor, "Growing Older: Finding Fulfillment in Art," *The Providence Sunday Journal*, June 19, 1983, p. C-4.

That Victory Garden, which was a common occurrence throughout the country, extended across the full width of the property behind our house. Farmhands came in the spring to plow and disc the garden and fertilize it with chicken manure, which was plentiful.

It is gratifying to learn that our huge garden area is now being utilized by the University of Rhode Island Master Gardeners Association in cooperation with the university's Cooperative Extension Education Service to create a demonstration vegetable garden. In addition, our old home serves as the field house for the program.

Photo 86: The Demonstration Vegetable Garden, 2024

Photo 87: View from the Master Gardener's Field House at East Farm

We were like an island within East Farm, surrounded by roads on all sides, which led to various poultry and horticultural buildings. East Farm fronted on the main highway, Route 108, and there were two paved roads that entered the property, separated by a large apple and peach orchard. Our home and yard were located quite a way back from the main highway.

In the garden, Dad grew tomatoes, corn, cucumbers, peas, green beans, lettuce, radishes, onions, potatoes, squash, watermelon, and probably more. Mom canned many fruits and vegetables, which we consumed all year long. I can remember wishing I'd never see another stewed tomato or green bean, but I never tired of the sweet pickles, pears, peaches, applesauce, and grape juice. Teresa especially remembers the grape juice paired with popcorn in the winter months. In those days, there were no fresh vegetables available in the winter. During one year, Dad tapped the maple trees to make maple syrup. That was an adventure, but it took forever for the syrup to boil down to the proper consistency in our huge roasting pan. The flavor was a bit odd, and certainly didn't measure up to the pure Vermont maple syrup that we could buy at the store. That had something to do with the weather conditions in Rhode Island. Maple syrup is better when it comes from trees further north. Or perhaps we just didn't have the right variety of maple trees.

Many food items were rationed during the war, and Mom split the sugar equitably among the five of us. Dad had a very hard time with his sugar allotment running short, while my sister and I hoarded ours until we had enough for baking something special, perhaps a cake or peppermint patties. Teresa remembers gloating when Dad's allotment was gone, and I probably felt the same way.

At Christmas time after the war, our parents would often give Teresa and me a gift of a leaf-shaped piece of maple sugar, which was—and still is—my absolute favorite sweet. I would make that one small piece of candy last for several weeks by only taking the tiniest bite each day. It had such an intense flavor. Then I would hide it behind the books in the living room. Candy was a very rare item in our household.

During the war, some of the coastline was off-limits with barbed wire strung in places and military encampments in place. On rare occasions, we would go to the movies, where there would be propaganda clips and newsreels about the battles abroad. I'm sure the constant propaganda, the massive bombings, the horror of the prison camps, and the political convictions of my parents all colored my outlook on the disaster and futility of war and the injustices felt by so many people.

For Dad's part, he wrote a letter to his father in 1945, saying that he was writing to his congressman to state that he was dead set against proposed legislation that would create a program of universal military training. In part of that letter, he said:

> *It will prove to be, if enacted, one of the costliest things the people of our nation have ever undertaken. I cannot see our country embarking upon a program which is essentially one of permanent war footing. I would like to see the administration drive hard for a good peace.*

And look at where we are now—on a permanent war footing.

Dad landscaped the front and back yards attractively. Two huge maple trees dominated the front yard, and there was a small rock garden in one corner where he planted many annuals and perennials. At the back of the house, he created a small picnic area that we called "the Nook." It had a fireplace and green Adirondack lawn chairs surrounded by shrubbery to make a cozy area that screened us from the rest of the farm.

Teresa remembers a little fishpond where a turtle hung out and maybe a duck. There were also a couple of other ducks, the white Donald Duck types, that roamed the immediate area. They disappeared at some point, and I always suspected that we ate them. After all, it *was* a farm. We played badminton and croquet on the large grassy backyard, where Dad also constructed a giant swing set. Sometimes we played Monopoly with Mom and Dad, or checkers with Dad. Teresa and I liked playing games outside. Dad even bought us baseball gloves and a football. I saw Larry as more a tinkerer than an athlete. But maybe he just didn't have support from Dad. In an e-mail to me, he wrote:

> *Dad and sports: There's a sore spot for me. Dad played golf—I think before WW II. He never shared a golf club with me. I can remember sitting in his car while he played near*

West Kingston. He tossed a ball [to me] a few times. I guess he thought I was too inept to continue. I think he played on a baseball team in Michigan, but know no details.

Teresa remembers Dad claiming to be a switch hitter, but would have played left-handed if allowed by the coach.

Teresa and I had a childhood friend, Sarah Greene, who sailed small catboats with her family on Salt Pond in Wakefield, and I was very envious of her, for I would have loved to learn how to sail. Larry wrote:

At one point, Dad was poised to buy a sailboat. He never did, but he sailed with others. I really believe privation weighed heavily with these decisions.

Oh, gosh, I remember that, and so hoped that Dad would buy that boat. But apparently it was too expensive.

During the summers, we swam at Larkin's Pond, which was about three miles from home. It was a delightful spot. I suppose Mom or Dad took us there for swimming lessons when we were young. Larry would ride his bike there with friends, but Teresa and I would walk there when we were older. Yes, six miles round trip. I suppose we didn't have bikes at the time. The water was not nearly as cold as the ocean, so we could actually swim in it. What we didn't like was the uphill walk back home in the hot, humid air. We also occasionally went to the beach on the coast, but transportation would have been an issue.

In 1945, Jay P., Dad's father, died. In a letter that Dad wrote to Teresa in September 1978, he described reading and filing his parents' letters.

I've spent all day and a part of yesterday putting Mother and Dad's letters with a few others in order in the file. It has been a very sad task. I had to give up reading the letters—the misery, the sickness, the poverty, the great courage gets to me. So, I proceeded by dates to file them in order. What for? I shall never read them again.

Dad went on to say that Jay P. was very lonely and grief-stricken after Mabel's death, when his health declined, and he grew very deaf.

He continued farming with the help of Dad's brother, Max, until he died in 1945. Max then inherited the farm and all the debt, plus Jay P.'s insurance, whose premium payments Dad had met for a number of years. But, as Dad said, "Max had earned it."

In fact, I think Dad actually resented that everything was left to Max, who lost the farm very soon after inheriting it. Dad said that if he had been included in the will, he would have saved the farm, and it would still be in the family. I shudder to think of it, because that might have meant a move to Michigan in 1945, when I was 10, and real farm life. But perhaps Dad wouldn't have been that rash. I'm sorry I never met Jay P. or any of my other grandparents or Uncle Claude. It seemed like we didn't have any relatives at all, certainly not nearby.

Dad continued to paint when he had time, making use of an old Quonset hut on the farm for his art studio. It sat behind the main Poultry Department building and was occasionally used for meetings. I call it a studio, but it was just an unused classroom, where Dad set up his easel and painting equipment.

Photo 88: The Quonset Hut As It Looked in 2024

Quonset huts were common on the main college campus after World War II, when they were used as classrooms, but I only remember one at East Farm. The lighting must have been miserable, since there was only one window at either end of the building. Dad tried to paint my portrait and Teresa's in there, but didn't complete them because he was unhappy with the results. That was a relief to both of us, because we didn't like to sit so long, posing for him.

The Farm

Across from our house, there was a building that had offices for the Poultry Department, the labs of the Animal Pathology Department, and the Poultry Hatchery. Dad's office was also in that building. How convenient it was for him to only have to walk across the road to his office. The staff included veterinarians, extension service personnel, and secretaries.

Photo 89: Dad Candling Eggs, ca. 1940

Photo 90: Some of the East Farm Staff, ca. Late 1940s

This photo of the poultry staff on a winter day is one of my favorites. I think that's me to the far left, but it could be my sister. Dad, in the white shirt, is tossing a snowball at Dr. William Wiley, the head of the Poultry Department. In the front, Frank Woodmansee is holding two baskets of eggs. Dr. Delaplane, whom I will mention later, is on the far left behind me.

Over the years, the farm expanded with added poultry and horticultural buildings. The Pomology Department staff, who studied fruit and its cultivation, planted trial orchards of cherries, plums, peaches, and pears. The cider from the apple orchards was wonderful, as my sister and I discovered by sneaking into the horticulture building after hours, where we found large wooden casks filled with it. I still have a hankering for that cider.

Photo 91: The Horticultural Building Where Teresa and Nancy Found Casks of Cider

Elsewhere on the farm, there were grapes, blueberries, and other fruits. One summer, Teresa and I picked strawberries and were paid five cents per box to do so. But it was back-breaking work and not worth the effort. I have great sympathy today for farmworkers.

On a warm summer night, there was nothing we liked better than to walk over to the orchard for a nice juicy fresh peach. On a rare occasion, Teresa and I would wander from one end of the farm to the other, sampling various fruits. We were always careful never to leave any evidence, so I don't suppose anyone ever knew. By around 5:00 P.M., all the farmhands had gone home, so we had the place to ourselves.

The farm seemed very large to us as children, and I suppose it was. It grew from an initial nine acres in 1930 to about seventy-five acres by 1951. We weren't really aware of that, since the nucleus of the farm stayed pretty much the same. In those years, we had freedom to explore it as much as we liked, so long as we were home for meals. I know that my sister and I wandered over every inch of the farm, and I'm sure our brother did as well. Sometimes, our travels took us into neighboring properties, through fields and woods, leaving us in unfamiliar territory. There were paths that led into woods on three sides of the farm, so occasionally we'd find ourselves behind someone's private property. At that point we'd head back. There was a small stream that crossed the property, and Teresa and I spent much time exploring its path and wishing it were wider. Unfortunately, it tended to dry up in the summer, which spoiled our fun. Since Larry was three years older than we were, our explorations did not include him. But we were always very curious, wondering what we would find beyond the next bend in the path.

I'm sure Larry was just as curious as we were. In fact, I recall him telling me about starting up one of the trucks after the farmhands had gone home, and banging into the door frame of the garage. So, we weren't the only ones causing trouble.

During the war, Dad raised a pig that he would later have butchered, keeping the meat in a rented refrigerated locker in town. He kept the pig in a shed that was attached to the barn behind our house. On one occasion, when my sister and I tried to ride the pig, it jumped out of a tiny window and headed for the woods. That forced Dad and the farmhands to spend quite a long time trying to corral her. Suspecting us, Dad was livid. But this is another case of shared guilt, since Teresa thinks that she was the one who tried to ride the pig, and I think I was. I wish I had fessed up to Dad as an adult to see his reaction. He probably would have laughed.

The very next day, that darn pig did it again *without* our instigation. But that probably saved our skin, because we were nowhere in sight that time.

As children, Teresa and I spent many hours with the farmhands, following them around as they worked. Ray Taylor, the poultry foreman of the farm, and Leon Round, a general farmhand, seemed to enjoy our presence. They would let us ride in the back of the pickup truck—until one day a branch caught us and scratched our faces. After that, there was no more riding in the back of the truck. What a bummer!

East Farm

Another farmhand I recall was Frank Woodmansee, who appeared to us to be as ancient as the hills—an old unapproachable "swamp Yankee." His answers were always a simple "yup" or "nope." He wasn't much for conversation. I remember his wife picking him up every afternoon after work in an ancient vehicle, which looked like it might require a crank to start it.

I'm sure all the farmhands kept an eye on us as we played farmers' helpers. East Farm was a wonderful place to raise a family. It had all the advantages of living on a farm without us having to do any of the work. The disadvantage was that Teresa and I had no playmates.

When Dad was out of town on business, it fell to Teresa and me to close the doors on the coops of the free-range chickens at dusk. Those were young chickens, which weren't yet laying eggs. There were about fifty of them per pen, but I don't remember how many pens there were, perhaps six. Each pen was enclosed with its own wire fencing. Once the chickens were about six months old, they were moved to the poultry houses, which had nesting boxes.

Whenever my sister and I closed the chicken coops, it was a little scary because we were always on the lookout for skunks, which tended to hunt for food around dusk. If the coops weren't shut up, the skunks could enter and kill the chickens. They could kill quite a few in a short time and then eat them. We weren't really afraid of the skunks; we just didn't want to get sprayed. We recall that happening to Dad one time.

Dad was a stickler for Teresa and me always acting in a proper manner. Most of all, he wanted us to wear dresses. Of course, dresses were required at school and even in college in the 1950s, but most of the time, to Dad's displeasure, we were in jeans—or "dungarees," as we called them back then. Dad's mantra was always, "What will people think?" We didn't care, but he sure did. We were happy when slacks became fashionable for women.

We had African American neighbors who lived across the road from the farm on Route 108. The grandparents lived in a very tidy, well-maintained home at the front of their property. In back of the house, there were a couple of rundown homes in which other families lived, named Robinson, Potter, and Walmsley. Perry Potter was my brother's best friend for a while. As preschoolers, he and Larry were a bit rambunctious. One day, they broke all the windows in a chicken house by throwing rocks at it. Larry can't remember his punishment, so it must have been mild.

Like us, the African American children went to Kingston Hill Grammar School, about a mile from our home, although they moved or dropped out long before eighth grade. It was a K-8 school, with four classrooms and a lunch room, so there were two grades in each classroom. One of the African American girls, whose name I think was Mildred, occasionally walked to school with us. She must have been about our age. I remember the other children were a little older.

A couple of times, Teresa and I played baseball with those kids in the upper pasture near the highway. It was fun and I looked forward to more playtime, since my sister and I didn't have any playmates. But that didn't last long, because someone at the farm decided that the "Negroes" shouldn't be allowed on the farm property, since they might steal something. I was crushed. It was so unfair. Teresa recalls being invited over to their house for cocoa one day. She said we should have reciprocated in kind, but we didn't. Instead, Mom sent us over with some cookies or cake.

Usquepaug

Sometime during the 1940s, Dad bought a large home in Usquepaug, about six miles from Kingston. It would have made a nice home, although it was quite isolated. I suppose Dad intended to move there some day, but initially he rented it out. The house had a wonderful staircase banister, which I was tempted to slide down. But I never did, because Dad might see me. I was about 9 at that time, and Larry must have been 12 or 13.

In a letter to me, Larry later recalled:

> *I remember rewiring two houses with Dad. One in Usquepaug and the other the Church manse [in Kingston]. I helped him drive a well point in the basement for water successfully. I*

loved the barn there—wish we could have moved there, but shared the anxiety of being far from Kingston village during gasoline rationing. I helped Dad mow the 6-acre pasture, full of clover. We made a lot of trips together to that place—then it was gone. Dad and I put a lot of labor in revamping the manse for the new minister. We did it all—wash, wallpaper, paint, you name it.

Teresa and I remember Dad painting the floors in Usquepaug with a special technique called "spatter painting," a floor treatment that was commonly found in summer cottages along Cape Cod during the Colonial Revival period of the early twentieth century. To spatter a floor, the painter holds a brush in one hand and strikes it sharply with a stick. The paint then flies wildly in small droplets over the floor. I recall the colors being red, blue, and yellow—mostly primary colors on a dark background, probably brown.

Eventually, Dad found dealing with tenants too troublesome—especially when one of them took all the plumbing fixtures with him when he moved out. Soon after that, Dad sold the place.

Photo 92: The House in Usquepaug

It was Larry's responsibility to mow the lawn at home, but Dad was never satisfied with the results. In Larry's words:

> *We had use of a big old heavy steel-wheeled Jacobson 2-cycle power lawnmower. It gouged the soil. I fought to keep it going, because I hated the heavy hand mower.*

I still remember those lawn conflicts. Teresa and I would sometimes follow Larry's mowing by trimming along the edges and flowerbeds to make them look better. We were trying to keep the peace, knowing that Dad would not be pleased with a sloppy job.

In a letter to me in 2014, Larry wrote:

> *My biggest Christmas gift was a Schwinn bike with a 3-speed shift (Sturmey-Archer-British). It carried newspapers and special delivery letters. I was forever repairing punctured tires, a broken light, pedals that would fall off, and loose bolts fore and aft. Could never maintain a working light. It almost met its demise one day when I fell off my bike, when hitting a tree, in front of the Fish House in Kingston, evulsing the nail of my right fourth finger.*

Dad gave us pet bantam chickens when we were young, perhaps for training to raise chickens as we got older. I think we had three, one a rooster called Chanticleer, probably named by Mom. Chanticleer is a common name for a rooster in fables and in Chaucer's Canterbury Tales. My sister wrote in a note to me:

> *Do you remember when Dad built the house for the bantams? He was sure good at building things. Did we want bantams, or was that his idea, and we took care of them? I remember once when the weather was frigid, one of the little banties was just about dead with the cold, and we took it into the house and warmed it up next to a hot iron.*

In back of the playhouse—or the "shack," as Larry called it—Dad built a chicken coop and later a rabbit hutch. When Teresa and I were in a 4-H club, we fed the animals and sold the eggs and rabbits to the local grocer. That didn't bring in much money, particularly the eggs, because as the price of eggs went up, so did the cost of grain. I would call that an early lesson in agricultural economics. Successful farming is a tough business and very hard work. I knew I never wanted to marry a farmer.

Larry had the use of Dad's octagonal barreled .22-caliber Winchester rifle, which held several rounds. In a letter to me, he explained:

> *It was pump action, as I recall. I guess that makes it a repeater used to shoot squirrels, woodchucks, and Norway rats. I was never very good. Dad never gave me much instruction that I can recall, but I think I got a rifle merit badge in Boy Scouts. Mom cooked a squirrel once. It wasn't very tasty.*

Apparently, we also ate a woodchuck once, as Larry recently reminded me:

> *While I was in grade school, Dad gave me his antique .22 caliber rifle. I practiced on woodchucks and henhouse rats. The rats always won, but at least one woodchuck did not and became an (ugh?) family meal.*

Teresa remembers Larry giving the woodchuck to Mom, who was a good sport. But I must say it was tasteless and barely edible.

Larry may not have been a good shot, but Dad was a deadeye. I remember an incident in the 1970s when Dad grabbed his Winchester and shot a rat on our patio from the upstairs bathroom window. One shot and that rat was a goner. My daughter, Chris, who was 3 at the time, was nearby and totally shocked. I think that's the only time I ever saw Dad shoot.

In 1944, there was a terrible hurricane, which took down multiple trees and tore the roof off of one of the long chicken houses at the farm, setting it down not far away. That was pretty astounding. Hurricanes, particularly along the coast, were dreaded events for adults, but for us children they were exciting. The great New England Hurricane of 1938, in which 682 people were killed, was still in people's memories, although not mine. While using his Boy Scout axe to trim branches from a fallen tree, Larry chopped a notch in the tibia of his left leg. Ouch! Perhaps that and other events caused Mom to write in her journal that "children were more a burden than a joy."

Chapter 7:
A Promise Kept

In 1944, after taking classes for several years at Rhode Island State College, Dad finally earned his bachelor's degree in General Agriculture. Mom had extracted a promise from him to finish college, but it took him sixteen years. They both must have been thrilled. He often said that if it were not for his 1936 pastel painting "The Vintage," he would not have earned his degree. That was the painting that impressed Dr. Weldin and Dr. Bressler so much that they encouraged Dad to finish college. They saw something in him, and that inspired him. To his father, Tom wrote:

> *I am enclosing a snapshot of us on the day of my graduation. You will see that the children are stretching up. I have always regretted that you have never seen the girls, and haven't seen Larry since he was a little tot. They are very bright and good children. Larry is very advanced for his years. Knows high school chemistry thoroughly now, and has quite a fund of knowledge in radio. If he keeps up, he will be a second Zed Atlee.[36] You would like your grandchildren, dad, especially the girls, for they are a good mixture of mother and Rachel.*

After Dad earned his degree in 1944, he was promoted to extension poultryman with teaching and research assignments. He claimed that one of his biggest fears was that his children would finish college before he did. The teaching assignments were probably limited to one or two classes per semester, since he was still expected to carry on with all his other duties as manager of the farm.

In a letter to his father in January 1945, Tom wrote:

---

[36] Zed Atlee was a cousin of Dad's. He was an engineer and a major contributor to the design of x-rays through improved instrumentation for crystal analysis.

I have been on a new job since the first of July and have had to work pretty hard. While, not by any means, did I think that after completing college training, that I would have to cease studying, I found that I would, rather, have to study harder than ever. Or to put it this way, instead of having the bull by the horns, I have a hold of the tail. My employers intend to get a day's work out of me. The new work is very enjoyable, so I don't mind.

His job status was a little odd, since part of his salary came from the college and part from the federal government, which funded the Agricultural Extension Service. The chairman of Dad's department was Professor Homer Stuart, whom Dad had known at the University of New Hampshire. They were very good friends. Homer smoked cigars and always had one chomped between his teeth. I don't believe he was ever invited into the house because of the stinking cigar.

Photo 93: Dad's Graduation Day, May 28, 1944

Homer and Dad loved to "jaw" together. After work, they would stand next to Homer's car in front of our house and talk for hours. I may be exaggerating, but as a kid I wanted Dad to come inside. An ironic twist is that Dad later bought Homer's 1942 Buick, which arrived with that horrible cigar smell. Some years later, to get rid of that smell, I reupholstered the interior, including the door panels, with a green vinyl. The usual saying is "Like father, like son." But my being handy was a case of "Like father, like daughter."

What excitement there was on the farm when Henry Wallace, FDR's second Vice President and former Secretary of Agriculture, visited the Egg-Laying Contest in 1944. I was 9 at the time and knew it was a big deal. Teresa remembers following Wallace around and being impressed by the State Troopers who guarded him in their highly polished brown leather boots, laced up to their knees. Dad was thrilled to talk with Wallace, and was in his element discussing production methods and disease control of chickens. In 1940, Wallace had developed commercial egg-layers, using the same genetic methods he had used earlier to successfully produce a hybrid form of corn. In 1936, he had started the Hy-Line Company, which produced baby chicks that were franchised all over the country. At one time, the Hy-Line Company's chickens produced three-quarters of all commercially sold eggs in the world.[37] What an astounding figure!

Dad also found time to do other interesting things, aside from farming. In a letter to his father, he said he enjoyed oil painting and wanted some day to do professional portrait painting, which had been a hobby of his for years. He formed a close friendship with our family pediatrician, Dr. Reuben Bates, and they visited art exhibitions together. Dad was also active in the community, belonging to the West Kingston Grange, the Hope Lodge #25 of the Masonic Order, the Kingston Improvement Association, the Tavern Hall Club, the Kingston Congregational Church, and the South County Art Association.

In the summer and fall of 1944, Mom was ill with a bladder infection. When her doctor told her that she needed complete rest, she took that

---

[37]John C. Cullver and John Hyde, *American Dreamer: The Life and Times of Henry A. Wallace* (New York: W.W. Norton, 2000).

literally, so Teresa and I had to fill the void. Dad wrote the following to his father:

> *Perhaps you have wondered how we have been getting along. Rachel has not been at all well and has been unable to do any housework for the greater part of the summer and fall. I do not know how we would have got along without the two fine little nine-year-old girls, who pitched in and did housework, such as cleaning, washing dishes, and even cooking at times. It was a hand-to-mouth existence for a while, and at the same time, I had to be out traveling over the state, carrying on the new job.*

He didn't mention the laundry, but we did that as well. I have no recollection of what Larry was doing during that summer, but he told me that he had a paper route and repaired radios in a shop. My keenest memory is of Mom sitting in a lawnchair, reading a book with a bottle of soda pop next to her, with Teresa and me as her servants. Soda pop was a very rare item at our home, so I suppose I was green with envy. It was one very long summer.

During the 1940s, my father continued to play the trumpet in the small South County Orchestra. He loved classical as well as marching band music. After he bought a monster-sized Arvin radio with shortwave bands late in World War II, loud music would blast forth from the record player on many a night. Dad would often entreat us to dance with him to a lively polka or waltz. In the summer, the speakers would be turned to face outside, so we could enjoy the music while barbecuing in "the Nook."

As children, we spent a lot of time listening to the radio, particularly *The Lone Ranger* and *The Shadow*. Those programs had to be turned off when Dad came home from work, since he didn't approve. During the summers, picnics on the granite coastal rocks off Newton Avenue in Narragansett were highlights for our family. The feeling of the fresh sea air on my face and the sound of the waves smashing against the rocks stay with me to this day. It's one place I always visit when I'm in Rhode Island.

Reminiscing about those years, Larry wrote:

> *During World War II, I was treated to Hawaiian guitar lessons at the Neighborhood Guild in Peace Dale. Dad would pick me up, and go to a church in Wakefield, and let me listen to the little orchestra where he played the trumpet. Hours of boring listening!*

Larry also remembers Dad practicing for Gilbert and Sullivan's operetta *Patience*, which was performed at Edwards Hall at the college, where many members of the orchestra were employees. Larry was away at school when the operetta was performed, so he missed it, and Teresa and I *never* saw Dad play the trumpet in public.

Photo 94: The Local South County Orchestra, ca 1940s
(Dad is standing at the far right, with May Steadman to his left and Dean Royal Wales in front with a cello)[38]

---

[38] May Steadman was a close family friend, and Royal Wales was the Dean of Engineering and a Professor of Mechanical Engineering at Rhode Island State College.

In 1946, my parents sent Larry to Mt. Hermon School for Boys in Gill, Massachusetts. Larry was very bright, and I have a feeling that my parents thought he might not fit in well at our local high school. I gleaned the following fascinating information from a doctoral dissertation on the history of Mt. Hermon School for Boys from 1881 to 1971. The school was founded in 1883 by Dwight L. Moody, a prominent evangelist of the nineteenth century. Previously, he had founded the Northfield School for Girls, in part because his own daughters needed a school. Both schools were created for poor students with limited access to education, with an emphasis on religion. Moody wanted to prepare evangelists to go out into the world.

At the time of its founding, Mt. Hermon School for Boys was not meant as a college preparatory school, and it had a very diverse population from its very beginning, including Native Americans, children of former slaves, and foreign students from around the world. In fact, in 1904, its 139 students came from 28 different countries. However, by the 1940s, when Larry attended, the emphasis had become more academic, and the student body was focused on preparing for college. The school still accepted poor and working-class students, but it slowly catered mostly to the well-heeled from across the country. Moody believed in a conservative Christian religious education, but by the time Larry attended the school, it had become increasingly theologically liberal. Manual work requirements for the students had been reduced, and intramural sports and activities with the nearby Northfield School for Girls had been added.[39]

Finances were tight for my parents, but they secured a scholarship from the Schepp Foundation. Before Larry left for school, Dad taught him how to iron pants, preserving the crease, as well as how to shine shoes. He also made Larry a brown suit, since chapel attendance was required. Larry said the homemade suit was a pretty good fit, and he never felt embarrassed while wearing it. The students were expected to

---

[39] Joseph Robert Curry, "Mount Hermon from 1881-1971: An Historical Analysis of a Distinctive American Boarding School," Ph.D. dissertation, University of Massachusetts, 1972.

put in ten hours per week working on the school farm, the power plant, the laundry, the kitchen, or the bathrooms. I recall Larry complaining that he had to clean toilets. According to Teresa, Dad thought that was pretty funny, since Larry was notoriously bad at doing chores at home.

Speaking of chores, Larry mailed his laundry home each week, so Teresa and I were often tasked with doing it. Teresa remembers having to iron Larry's shirts. There was a laundry at Larry's school, but it was probably cheaper to mail his clothes home. Larry had two breaks during the year, at Christmas and Easter, for which he usually thumbed a ride home. In an e-mail about this to me, he wrote:

> *Well, I did it several times. It was an all-day affair. It's amazing I even tried, given the very indirect routing involved. I think I went through Springfield one time and took the train to Gill, the train stop, followed by a 5-mile walk to the campus. Else it was multiple brief rides up through Southbridge, etc.*

It was a bit like the old Maine saying, "You can't get there from here." When I asked Larry if Dad ever drove him to school, he replied:

> *Yes, he routinely drove me back. Even then—5 hrs (35 mph wartime speed limit everywhere).*

One year at Christmas break, Larry came home with an assignment, about which he wrote to me the following:

> *I was sent home from school with a soccer ball and told to make a silver (aluminum foil) rotating ball for a class dance party. Dad helped assemble the monster—a motor with a reduction gear in an apple box—and sewed the foil-covered soccer ball. We hung it over the dance floor. Grotesque!*

During that break, Larry sang in the Episcopal church for choir director T. Stephen Crawford, who was the Dean of the Engineering School at the University—and later, as we shall shortly see, a thorn in Larry's side. Teresa and I welcomed the respite from big brother's teasing. I know we visited Mt. Hermon a couple of times, but I don't recall much about the school. What I do remember seeing on one of those trips was a sign on a bed and breakfast that Mom pointed out, which said, "Gentiles Only." How appalling. That was in the 1940s, when such signs were still evident.

Photo 95: Mom, Teresa, Nancy, and Larry, ca. 1946
(Dad made Larry's suit and the twins' treasured corduroy Eisenhower jackets)

Dad traveled to many farms, giving advice on poultry management and disease control. To enable him to do this, the government gave him an extra gas allotment during the war. There were times when Dad would take Teresa and me on his farm trips, which caused us to occasionally miss grade school. I'm not sure why he did that, but it was fun. Perhaps we livened up his long drives, and he loved to show off his twins, whether we were out shopping or at church. Mom said we were in great demand as flower girls at weddings, but neither Teresa nor I remember that. Maybe Mom turned down the requests. When we were teenagers, we were expected to serve punch and cookies at faculty receptions.

A Promise Kept

Photo 96: Teresa and Nancy with Mary Endo, Ready to Serve Guests, ca. 1940s

Poultry Disease Research

One of the highlights of Dad's career was his collaboration in 1945 with Dr. John Delaplane in the discovery of the use of Sulfaquinoxaline for the control of avian coccidiosis and fowl cholera, perhaps saving the poultry industry at the time.[40] Coccidiosis is a parasitic disease of the intestines of humans, birds, and livestock, and fowl cholera is a contagious bacterial disease of birds. This discovery led the way to an explosive growth in the poultry industry worldwide. President Carl Woodward of the University of Rhode Island noted that industry savings from this research had an economic value that greatly exceeded

---

[40]Sandy Sawtelle, "R.I. Man's Research Assured 'Chicken in Every Pot,'" *Providence Evening Bulletin*, November 16, 1971, p. 28.

the entire cost of running the Experiment Station for the previous fifty years.[41] Dr. Delaplane and Dad also inaugurated a statewide program of immunization to control infectious bronchitis in poultry. The immunization and low-level medication programs they developed in the late 1940s are still closely followed today.[42]

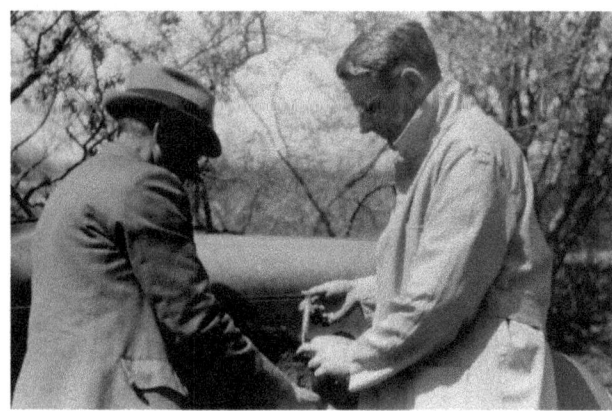

Photo 97: Dad (on the left) and Dr. Delaplane Inoculating a Chicken

During World War II, there was a shortage of beef, so efforts were begun to breed a better chicken. Prior to the war, chickens for eating were a by-product of the egg-laying industry. A bird was generally not butchered until her egg-laying days were over. The A&P Food Markets sponsored a competition among poultry breeders, in partnership with the United States Department of Agriculture, to produce a chicken with more meat on it. Almost every state participated, and Dad became state chairman of the Chicken of Tomorrow Contest for Rhode Island. Competitions spread across the states, and in 1948 there was a national competition. Those contests resulted in better quality chickens for roasting and frying.

---

[41] The University of Rhode Island, *Detailed History*, available at https://www.uri.edu/about/history/detailed-history/.

[42] Henry F. Reilly, "R.I. Farm News: Poultrymen to Honor Prof. Higgins," *Providence Evening Bulletin*, January 11, 1965, p. 7.

Photo 98: *A Family Picnic in Our Backyard*
(Dr. and Mrs. Delaplane are standing between Mom and Dad, and the Delaplane girls are seated on either side of the twins)

Dad also became a member of the first committee to explore the interior quality of eggs. Originally, farmers candled eggs to explore their interior in order to determine their freshness and to look for blood spots and other abnormalities. The word *candling* comes from the original use of candles to examine eggs. Today, eggs are held up to a very strong electric light to reveal their insides. Their quality is then graded based on the size of the small air sac, the clarity and firmness of the egg white, and how well-defined the egg yolk is. Any eggs with blood or meat spots are considered inedible. Candling is also used to determine if the egg is fertile, and I suppose that might be why the Poultry Department gave us so many leftover eggs. I remember a gallon of raw eggs sitting in our refrigerator from time to time. And we ate *many* of them with blood spots! (By the way, they tasted just like any other eggs.)

Photo 99: Mom and Dad Cooking a Chicken on a Spit

The first large poultry operations in the country were located in Little Compton, the birthplace of the Rhode Island Red chicken. As a poultry specialist with the Agricultural Extension Service, Dad traveled throughout the state, talking to local poultry groups and helping farmers with whatever problems they had in the production of eggs and poultry. He trained and coached winning Future Farmers of America; 4-H egg and poultry judging teams at the Eastern States Exposition in West Springfield, Massachusetts; and egg and poultry judging teams at the Northeastern Poultry Producers Council egg-grading school in Harrisburg, Pennsylvania.

Dad also authored or co-authored over thirty scientific publications. The only one I have seen is a 24-page pamphlet called *4-H Poultry and Egg Marketing*.[43] The pamphlet covers everything from egg quality and egg grading to killing and plucking chickens for market, as well as

[43]Thomas C. Higgins., *4-H Poultry and Egg Marketing*, Bulletin 150, Extension Service, University of Rhode Island, Kingston, RI, March 1953.

figuring out a selling price. The information in it is still relevant today for backyard chicken growers.

In the 1930s and 1940s, the Poultry and Pomology Departments at East Farm put on barbecues and clambakes for people in their industries, to which government officials often came. The Poultry Department continued its barbecues into the 1950s. Those became large events, at which Teresa and I would always be lingering nearby to watch the festivities. There was one day that I was asked to help set up the tables. I don't recall that, but Teresa reminded me that I was paid five dollars for my efforts. Teresa wasn't chosen to help me, perhaps because people felt sorry for her after she knocked out her two front teeth when she flew over the handlebars of her bike. She said she was extremely jealous of me, as well she should have been, because $5.00 was a lot of money for a 10-year old in those days. In fact, in 2024 that would be equivalent to $84.00.

Photo 100: A Fruit Growers' Meeting at East Farm, ca. 1930[44]

Losing her teeth was not Teresa's only mishap that year. She also had a run-in with that wretched wringer washing machine when we

---

[44]University of Rhode Island Archives and Distinctive Collections, photo, 1930.

helped Mom one day with the laundry. At that time, we would agitate the dirty clothes in the washing machine tub and then feed them through the wringer to extract the dirty water. The clothes would land in a set tub filled with clean rinse water. Then we would swish them around by hand and put them through the wringer again. At some point in this process, Teresa leaned in too close to the wringer, and a large patch of hair was pulled out from the top of her head. I cringe at the thought. It was probably a four-inch circle. When I mentioned it to her recently, she said:

> *It hurt plenty, but just momentarily. I remember going to school with the missing hair on display, but I just needed to comb it on the other side. Maybe I wanted to show it off along with my broken front teeth.*

Teresa and I think so much alike that I don't think we've ever fought or argued about anything to this day. That worried Mom, who decided that we must have repressed our feelings and needed to express them. So, when we were about 14, she bought us boxing gloves! Come to think of it, that's a real contradiction to Mom's feelings about nonviolence. Teresa remembers that we boxed in the basement of the office building across from our house, sometimes with an audience—probably just Dad and maybe a farmworker or two. We didn't have any anger to express, but we had fun trying to bang each other up with the gloves. I think we got tired of it pretty quickly, but the word got out somehow, and we were teased about it at school. We only learned about Mom's intent when we were older. However, I don't think we had repressed feelings, nor were we ever particularly competitive. We were equally capable in whatever we did and tried to always do our best. One of our teachers had us retake a test one time because she thought we had cheated, since our scores were identical. We proved her wrong.

In 1950, Larry returned home from prep school to attend Rhode Island State College, which became the University of Rhode Island in 1951. He really wanted to become an engineer, but Dr. Crawford, the Dean of Engineering, his former choir director, discouraged him from doing so. He would have made a fine engineer, but instead chose to be a physician, partly inspired by Dr. Delaplane, the veterinarian who had collaborated with Dad on poultry diseases.

Photo 101: Nancy, Teresa, and Larry at Gettysburg

Teresa and I attended South Kingstown High School in Wakefield, a three-mile ride by school bus. That was the period when Dad made our beautifully tailored and lined woolen suits. The finishing touch was an embroidered label on the inside with his name on it. Those suits were perfect and looked very sharp. I think Dad was a perfectionist, although he never imposed his standards on us. In fact, I don't recall his ever criticizing us about *anything*, except for the fact that he preferred us to wear dresses rather than jeans. We knew he wanted us to do our best, and we always tried to please him. Mom also had her standards, which related to housecleaning. We always had chores to complete on the weekend, and dusting was at the head of the list.

*Photo 102: Teresa and Nancy Wearing Their New Suits
(across from the Kingston Congregational Church)*

Photo 103: Dad's Clothing Label, ca. 1950

Photo 104: Teresa, Mom, Larry, and Nancy, ca. 1955
(Note the low ceiling in the living room and the twins' suits made by Dad)

Photo 105: Larry's Mighty Moe's Ice Cream Truck, ca. 1955

As I have said, Teresa and I were not really competitive, but we always strived to get perfect grades—and, in fact, we had identical grades except for our toughest class, Physics. In that class, I was ahead of her by about half a point on one test. I wasn't really aware of that until the principal told me that I had earned the Bausch & Lomb Science Award for having the highest science grade average in our senior class. Because of that, the "powers-that-be" decided that perhaps Teresa should be the valedictorian to even out the awards. The principal ran that plan by us to get our agreement. I remember being a little miffed at the lack of acknowledgment, but secretly relieved at not having to give a speech.

In 1953, Teresa and I joined Larry at the University of Rhode Island, although we barely crossed paths with him there. He graduated in 1954 and went on to Tufts Medical School in Boston. In that same year, Dad resumed his advanced studies in Agricultural Economics. Working on his Master's degree was an ordeal for him, or at least it seemed so to me, since his advisers were constantly returning his thesis to him for changes, which irritated him. Perhaps academic writing was not his forte. I think those struggles colored my own thoughts about getting an advanced degree, although I did consider Library Science at one point.

While Larry was a college student, he bought an old Model A Ford for $150, which he named "Henrietta." It required a lot of maintenance, for which Larry was often assisted by Henry Durant, a middle-aged farmhand who lived in the Egg-Laying Contest building on the farm. Larry said that Henry was hardworking, kind, and gentle, so he named the car after him. It was very convenient for Larry to have someone living at the farm who was highly skilled in engine mechanics. I recall Henry helping Larry to do a valve job and other repairs. About those experiences, Larry wrote:

> *Dad was very supportive when the car's main bearing gave out. He arranged for someone in Providence to pour and align-bore the bearing, but I paid for the work. The fix lasted a year and got done again, along with valve grinding—the latter achieved by Henry and me. In 1931, crankshafts were not dynamically balanced; thus wear happened with ordinary use.*

Henry and Larry painted the car a gorgeous green, which made it look splendid. I was a little jealous because I didn't own a car at that time.

Also, when Larry was in college, he and a friend, Fred Schreiber, were caught racing their Model A's up Kingstown Road. In those days, there was very little traffic, although today it's nonstop. Larry remembers about this incident:

> *Dad was amused that Fred and I could go that fast. Or maybe he was proud. I was driving with the Model A wide open with*

wheels shimmying at maybe 50 mph. Police Chief Walter McNulty was amazed at our speed, and he cautioned us to drive a bit slower!

Dad's Interest in Paranormal Phenomena

One of the paranormal phenomena that Dad was most interested in was extrasensory perception (ESP). One day, because Teresa and I are identical twins, he put some cards with symbols on them in front of us in the dining room to test for psychic traits. But the tests proved inconclusive. We were probably around 7 at the time. When I asked Teresa about it, she said:

> *Oh, my gosh! I think you're right about us sitting at the dining room table. I remember being disappointed that we didn't live up to Dad's expectations. I'm not sure how he tested us. I don't think we challenged each other. We certainly weren't very old. Seems to me, it was sort of boring.*

Dad's study of water dowsing led him to experiment with various materials for dowsing rods, as well as with different methods of holding the rods, so that he couldn't influence their movement. Traditionally, people used wishbone-shaped sticks. I recall Dad pacing around the yard with wooden sticks or coat hangers. He even placed the ends of the sticks in test tubes to insulate them, but the sticks still turned down. Using dowsing rods, he successfully found water for our well in the backyard, but he kept that skill pretty much to himself. I suppose he didn't want other people to rely on his hunches. Today, dowsing is a widely debunked method for finding water, but is still used by many farmers.

Dad's most controversial interest in bizarre subjects involved the theories and devices developed by Dr. Wilhelm Reich, especially his orgone accumulators, which Reich believed could provide a treatment for cancer and other medical conditions by collecting "orgone energy," also known as *chi*, or life energy. However, whenever Dad discussed this subject with Mom, they got very hush-hush, so I only heard snippets of their conversations here and there.

Sometime in the 1950s, Dad and a professor of psychology drove up to Maine to visit the Institute for Orgonomic Science, but Reich wasn't there at the time, which was a big disappointment to Dad. Nevertheless, when he came home, he built his own orgone accumulator—I believe for the purpose of poultry research.

Photo 106: Dad Dowsing with a Tree Branch Near the House

Reich's work was eventually debunked by the Food and Drug Administration, which issued an injunction against him, claiming that he had delivered "misbranded and adulterated" devices in interstate commerce, and made false and misleading claims about those devices, which the agency insisted had to be destroyed. In 1956, the agency accused Reich of violating the injunction. He was arrested and died in prison in 1957. Reich stipulated in his will that his papers be sealed for fifty years after his death.[45] Today, there is a Wilhelm Reich Museum in Rangely, Maine, and his papers are at the Library of Congress in Washington, DC, as well as in the Countway Library of Medicine at Harvard University.

Photo 107: The Rhode Island Red[46]

---

[45]Mary Bellis, *Wilhelm Reich and the Orgone Accumulator.* Available at https://www.thoughtco.com/wilhelm-reich-and-orgone-accumulator-1992351/.

[46]Rhode Island Red Centennial Committee, *A History of the Rhode Island Red, 1854-1954* (Providence: State of Rhode Island and Providence Plantations, 1954).

Back to Chickens

In 1954, Dad was a member of the Rhode Island Red Centennial Committee, which promoted and secured the adoption of the Rhode Island Red as the state bird. Dad was very proud of that accomplishment. The chicken was bred in the second half of the nineteenth century by crossing birds of Asian origin with brown Leghorn birds from Italy in Little Compton, Rhode Island This was done for two purposes: eggs and meat. In the 1940s and 1950s, Rhode Island had a large poultry industry, and most of the birds at East Farm were Rhode Island Reds. The State of Rhode Island celebrated the centenary of the bird in 1954 by placing a monument in the town of Adamsville, just northeast of Little Compton. It was nice to see "our" bird chosen, and I still wear an R.I. Red pin on my jacket.

Photo 108: My Rhode Island Red Pin

Flying the Coop

In 1954, when Teresa was 19 and a sophomore in college, she and her boyfriend, Arthur Hathaway, unbeknownst to the rest of the family, were thinking of getting married. Dad was totally frustrated when he somehow discovered the plan. Art apparently was looking for an apartment, which could have triggered some comment to Dad. It was a small town and gossip flies. Teresa doesn't have a clue how Dad found out, but she said she had no interest in eloping. Dad was furious because he wanted Teresa to finish college. In those days, if a girl got married, that almost always meant that she would drop out of college. The tension in the house became almost unbearable for me, but I think Teresa was oblivious to it all because she spent most of her time with Art.

After a great deal of consternation, Mom and Dad persuaded them to wait for a year, during which they allowed Teresa to live on campus. Lucky Teresa! I wish *I* had been able to live on campus. Arthur graduated a year later, in 1955, and he and Teresa got married that September. She wanted to finish her degree and was searching for colleges to attend. When I asked her why so many of her choices were in Ohio, she responded:

> *This may seem crazy, but we knew we wanted to go fairly far away from home. I looked at the different states, and counted how many colleges they had. Ohio had the most. I don't remember if that was total or just small colleges. I knew I didn't want to go to a big school. So that led me to Heidelberg. It was a good choice for Art too, since he was able to find a good job as a draftsman the first day.*

When she asked our minister, Rev. John D. Beck, what he knew about Heidelberg College, he said he thought it was on a par with Oberlin. That was a good recommendation. Teresa's moving away was a huge loss for me.

Exodus from the Farm

In anticipation of owning our own home in the future, Dad bought property on Kingstown Road, not far from East Farm. The first thing he did was to use his dowsing expertise to locate a spot for a well. Then he acquired copies of house plans for one of the older colonial homes in Kingston, which was owned by a well-known book illustrator, Helen Gross. Because the property was swampy, a few of Dad's friends thought he was nuts to build there, but Dad felt otherwise. By grading the land toward the little brook that ran through the middle of the property and raising the level of the site of the future house, he avoided *most* of the water problems—although he later had to install a sump pump for the occasional flooding from hurricanes.

Dad hired contractors to frame the house, and I think also to build the fireplace, put up the walls, finish the roof, and shingle the exterior. Then he went on to do the major parts of finishing the interior, which included plastering the walls, building bookshelves in the library, and installing cabinets in the two bathrooms. He hired subcontractors to do the plumbing and electrical work. He also handcrafted crown molding for each room as well as the fireplace mantel with its vertical supports. In the living room, he installed chair rails with plaster walls below and grasscloth wallpaper above, which gave the room a very warm and cozy feeling.

Construction was well under way when Dad's boss told him that he had to move sooner than he expected. Mom and Dad had lived at East Farm for twenty-six years, when they got that news with very little notice. The sudden move caused untold headaches, since Dad had to work hard to make the new house livable. First of all, he hastily built and installed the kitchen cabinets of knotty pine. One of the last things he did was to install the hardwood floors in our bedrooms. At that point, although Dad was still teaching part-time and also working as an extension poultry specialist at the university, he still maintained his office at the farm.

I don't know why we were suddenly evicted after twenty-six years, but as my brother put it:

> *Dad would say, "Our residence there must have been a little burr in someone's saddle."*

Although Dad was essentially a caretaker of the farm, it was quite a perk to live in a house for so many years without having to pay for rent or utilities.

After we moved into the new home, Dad painted and wallpapered the whole house. He made beautiful full-length floral drapes for the living room and library, and essentially decorated the whole place. I don't think Mom had very much input in the design. She told me when she was in her late 80s that she never liked the grasscloth wallpaper.

During any spare time that I had from college, I helped Dad at the new house, hauling large rocks to place along the meandering brook that flowed through the property, and painting the pine bookshelves in the library with a sealer. I remember the noxious fumes that emanated from that project, since there were no fans anywhere.

Dad landscaped the yard beautifully, planting many shrubs and trees. In front of the house, where the yard sloped down toward the highway, he planted rhododendrons and blueberry bushes. The rhododendrons surrounded the blueberry bushes, so that they could not be seen from the road and picked clean by strangers. The lot was quite large, so there was a big expanse of grass to mow, most of it in the shade from existing trees.

Mom, Dad, and I moved into the new home in 1956. Much work still needed to be done, but it was livable. Incidentally, the old farmhouse sat unused for at least two years after we moved out. Bureaucracy moves in strange ways.

Photo 109: Our New Home, Dad's Pride and Joy

Dad, now in his mid-fifties, always kept busy with his many interests. He no longer had the large garden but instead, a large landscaped yard which was demanding. He still had time to try his hand at other things. He made several braided rugs for the new home. I believe they were considered fashionable in colonial style homes. He probably read a book on how to make them or learned from friends. It was a popular hobby at that time. He also crafted a beautiful rosewood cabinet for hi-fi equipment using wood from an old piano. With his careful attention to detail, he seemed to excel at whatever he tried.

Photo 110: Dad Tending to the Fireplace, 1965

With a major in Textiles and Clothing, I chose a senior project at college to weave a colonial-style linen and woolen bedspread on a large nineteenth-century four-harness loom. Dad and I moved the loom, which I borrowed from my professor, Dr. Marion Fry, to my bedroom. I don't know how on Earth I had the patience to set up the linen threads for the pattern of the warp. It was very complex. Once the warp was in place, I began to weave the navy wool yarn through the threads. It was a thrill when I started to see the pattern emerge. The loom only accommodated a thirty-five-inch width, so that meant I had to weave a double length and then piece the two together. Oh, my! I should have opted for a child's bedspread. Every time I thumped on the treadles, I think Dad cringed, fearing that the new living room ceiling below would crack. In fact, I tried to keep my weaving hours to those when he was not at home. What an undertaking, but no cracks in the ceiling ever developed. I thought the project would never end. My professor gave me a fancy four-inch fringe to attach to the edges, which added a nice touch. However, the bedspread has been wrapped up in a box, hidden away, for most of the last sixty-four years, because it's really not wide enough for today's double beds, and not many people have single beds these days.

Photo 111: Nancy's Senior Project, a Handwoven Bedspread

A Blind Date and a Long Wait

I met Donald Hall on a blind date during my freshman year in college. I loved that he played the piano and was so gregarious. Sadly for me, he left college after only two years to join the military. But in August 1957, when he finished his Army service, we were married. I think I barely knew him, since he had been overseas in Germany for two years.

Not to be outdone by his two sisters, my brother married his fiancé, Marian Hess, two weeks before my wedding. What a trial for Mom and Dad! A whirlwind of two weeks, but Mom was happy that she could wear the same dress for both weddings.

Dad was a staunch advocate of attending college. In 1956, he received his Master of Science degree in Agricultural Economics from the University of Rhode Island and was still afraid that Teresa would not finish her degree. But he need not have worried, since she and I both finished our degrees in 1957—she with a degree in Mathematics from Heidelberg College, and I with a degree in Textiles and Clothing from the University of Rhode Island. Some family members would say that Dad hounded his grandchildren to attend college, and most of them did.

Don and I lived in Kingston during our first two years of marriage, just at the edge of campus. I was fortunate to find a job in the University Library in Green Hall, while Don worked on completing his business degree. At the time, we had a 1953 Volkswagen sedan, which Don had shipped back from Germany at the government's expense. VW's were a rare sight in those days, so we would usually honk or wave if we saw another one. Because of its green color, we called it the "Pea Pod." One day, when Don and I were talking about how neat it would be to have a VW bus or van to go camping, Dad responded, "But you wouldn't want to drive that to church, would you?" Appearances! Appearances! Buying a VW bus was beyond our means, but Dad's response amused us. He was always concerned about the family's image.

Shortly after Don and I got married, my parents visited our apartment. Out of the corner of my eye, I caught a glimpse of Dad checking the tallest piece of furniture in the living room to see if I had dusted it.

Fortunately, I passed the test. Apparently, Teresa had experienced the same test. Dad expected perfection, so my sister and I provided it from almost perfect grades to perfect dusting.

Larry graduated in 1958 from Tufts Medical School, fulfilling Dad's dream of his son becoming a doctor. I'm not sure Dad had a dream for his twin daughters. Perhaps just a good marriage. Maybe some guidance would have been helpful, but Teresa and I were pretty independent. Dad showed us off incessantly from childhood to adulthood, which became very tiresome. I suppose that is why neither of us ever craves the limelight. When we were young, we were two cute peas in a pod. Later, Dad was proud of us because we brought home good grades. Kingston was a small town, and we were the only identical twins there, so for a long time many people immediately knew who we were.

It isn't often that Teresa and I are seen together now, since we live almost 900 miles apart, but when we are together, there are often inquisitive comments. Not too long ago, we even had a young man ask to take our picture when we were shopping. We often unintentionally dress in similar clothes, so it's not surprising that people notice us. We don't mind it now because it's so infrequent.

The Lure of the West

Teresa and Art moved to Northern California when Art got a job as a park naturalist at Muir Woods National Monument. After a year, they moved to Joshua Tree National Park in Southern California, where they stayed for about two years. Mom and Dad visited them and their first grandchild, and then toured some of the rest of the state. As they were extolling the beauty of California, Don and I dropped the bombshell on them that we were planning to move to San Francisco. Don had wanted to switch his major from business to music, but the Dean of the university, "Bulldog" Browning, would not allow the change. There wasn't much freedom of choice in those days. So, we scoped out various colleges, and found that San Francisco State had a well-respected music department and low tuition. Don was happy to move to California after working for his uncle, Stewart Bedell, in Big Pine for a summer. He loved the lack of humidity. I had worked one summer at a camp in the hills of San Bernadino, so I also knew the attractions of the state. But Mom and Dad were very sad when they heard our news.

In 1959, Don and I moved to San Francisco, where he continued his college studies, and I found a job in the San Francisco State College Library. Don switched from majoring in business to music, his passion. In a way, he went on to emulate Dad, because it was eleven years before he finally obtained his degree in music education.

At that time, Larry was fulfilling his military requirements in Las Cruces, New Mexico. After that, he and Marian moved several times before landing in San Antonio, where he set up his medical practice. Teresa and Art moved about ten times, since he was with the National Park Service. Their final destination was Cheney, Washington, not far from Spokane. Mom and Dad were left alone, and I know it was particularly hard on Dad to have his family so distant. Mom later told me that Dad was devastated to have all three children scattered to the winds. Don and I tried to visit Mom and Dad every couple of years, and they in turn made several trips west. They even drove across the country once, sleeping in the car to save money. Ever so frugal, or maybe adventuresome.

By 1968, Mom and Dad had ten grandchildren scattered around the country. Teresa and Art had four: Robert, Patricia, Nancy, and David. Larry and Marian had four: Laurel, Heather, Camille, and Thomas. And Don and I had two: Christine and Jeffrey. There are now countless grandchildren and great grandchildren. Mom called them her "little United Nations family." Out of ten grandchildren, four married people from different races or cultures: African American, Indian, Kenyan, and Korean. Recently, a great-granddaughter married a Vietnamese fellow. So, it would appear that there is a spirit of inclusiveness in my family.

Mom and Dad had many friends, whom they entertained frequently. There were a number of foreign students who studied at or visited the university in various capacities, and Dad was always quick to invite them to the house. Mom and Dad particularly enjoyed meeting twin boys from Mexico, whom they later visited on a trip to Mexico City.

Photo 112: Dad Holding Nancy's Daughter, Christine, in 1967

Barbecue Expert

Now and then, Mom sent news clippings to Larry, Teresa, and me, especially when Dad was featured. These would often be articles about chicken barbecues at East Farm, which the Poultry Department continued to hold over the years. Dad became very proficient at running those events, as the following article in *The Providence Journal* confirms:

> *The word has spread throughout the state and into Connecticut and Massachusetts that if you are making plans for a big chicken barbecue, Thomas C. Higgins, soft-spoken Extension Poultry Specialist at the University of Rhode Island, is your man. Tom's specialty has been big chicken barbecues for a few hundred people, but he is nonetheless an expert at the backyard or picnic variety.*[47]

Photo 113: A Cartoon by Paule Loring of Dad and Violet Higbee Barbecuing[48]

Those few hundred people were mainly regional poultry producers. Dad said that he "borrowed" a lot of ideas from other people along the way. At first, he put the chickens on individual spits. Later, at a

---

[47] Leonard O. Warner, "URI Poultryman Making Chicken Barbecue Popular," *The Providence Journal*, July 20, 1953, p. 20.

[48] "URI Experts Give Fine Points on the Backyard Barbecue," *The Providence Sunday Journal*, June 27, 1954, p. 16.

friend's suggestion, he placed perhaps as many as fifteen half-chickens between two layers of fox wire, so he could turn them all at once. He and Violet B. Higbee, a nutrition specialist at the university, developed a barbecue sauce that was based on a hot Louisiana recipe. That sauce put the finishing touches on Dad's reputation.

Bosses Can Be a Pain

I don't know if Dad was a happy man in his later years. I think he may have suffered from depression at times. When Don and I would visit, I sometimes sensed a tension in the air, which I felt was work-related. I know he enjoyed working with farmers around the state, but I don't think he very much enjoyed working in the office. Mom indicated in her journal that he had a difficult relationship with his boss:

> *Tom had many problems with his boss, who seemed to want to hold him down, as three presidents and the dean of agriculture wanted to push him ahead.*[49]

Fraternity Woes

Dad had many irons in the fire, so to speak. One of those was his involvement with the administration and maintenance of Phi Gamma Delta, a fraternity at the university. During World War II, the house had been commandeered to be used as the University Student Union. After the war, the building needed a lot of work to make it habitable again for the fraternity brothers. Dr. Reuben Bates, our former pediatrician in the 1930s, inveigled Dad to become involved. Dr. Bates was chairman of the Beta Phi Corporation board, which owned the fraternity. It was an irritant to Mom that Dr. Bates took so much of Dad's time. I don't know what was involved, but it took Dad away from home for many hours. That started before Larry became a member of the fraternity and continued long after. It became a family effort at one time, since Teresa and I remember mowing the fraternity's lawn one summer when the regular mower was unavailable to clean up the premises after a hurricane.

---

[49]Rachel S. Higgins, unpublished journal, ca. 1990.

Photo 114: Dad and Mom, ca. 1974

Chapter 8:
New Endeavors

In 1964, after thirty-four years at the university, when Dad retired with the title of Professor Emeritus, his tension seemed to melt away. Throughout his career, he had been active in many industry-connected activities, including teaching poultry marketing. Among his greatest pleasures had been coaching the winning 4-H and Future Farmers of America egg- and poultry-judging teams at the Eastern States Exposition in Springfield, Massachusetts, and other similar events in Harrisburg, Pennsylvania.

But he didn't retire completely. He became President of the Board of Wardens, which oversaw the Kingston Volunteer Fire Department, where Larry had been a volunteer fireman when he was a student at the University of Rhode Island. I'm not sure what Dad's new job entailed—perhaps the business end of things. Kingston still has a volunteer force that provides protection for the University of Rhode Island as well as the town of Kingston. I don't think Dad ever went out to fight a fire, although I do remember his great mirth in telling the story of helping a portly woman out of a tub. That may or may not have been connected to the fire department.

In addition to becoming a fire warden, Dad took a part-time job as the manager of the Kingston Water Department during a period of rapid town expansion. One of his assignments included supervising the construction of a new water tower to supply the village. In the 1960s, he was also involved in developing housing in the Biscuit City area of Kingston, where the water company sold about thirty house lots. Kingston's water supply had come from the Biscuit City Pond until the

1960s, when the new water tower was built in town. In appreciation of Dad's contributions, the town named one of the streets Higgins Drive.⁵⁰

Photo 115: Dad (far right), ca. 1964

Biscuit City has an interesting history. I don't believe it ever had more than six homes. Kingston had been primarily a farming community of wealthy landowners, who were reluctant to industrialize the area. In the late 1700s, taking advantage of the natural spring in Biscuit City, a grist mill was built about a mile west of the center of town. Later, in the early 1800s, a cotton mill called the Cotton Manufactory was constructed by a corporation of twenty-six local men from South County, who hoped to build a manufacturing site close to Kingston. This is said to have been the first corporation in New England—but it did not prosper.⁵¹

A myth says that a peddler went to all the homes in Biscuit City, but none of the women would talk to him, since they were busy making

---

⁵⁰Arnold W. Peterson, "Tom Higgins: A 20th-Century Renaissance Man," *Narragansett Times*, September 28, 1990, pp. 3A-10A.]

⁵¹Christian M. McBurney, *A History of Kingston, R.I., 1700-1900: Heart of Rural South County* (Kingston, RI:, Pettasquamscutt Historical Society, 2004).

New Endeavors

biscuits. When he complained about this in a local tavern, the name stuck. However, the fact is that no one really knows why the small area is called Biscuit City, since it was never a city. None of the old buildings remain, and the pond and the surrounding area, about 10.5 acres in Biscuit City, has become part of the South Kingstown Land Trust.

Photo 116: Dad's Official Retirement Photo

The Travel Bug

Unbelievably, in 1965, about a year after Dad retired, he did something totally out of character for him. Inspired by some Egyptian friends at the university, the Dardiris, he took out a loan for him and Mom to make a trip to Egypt. He was partly motivated by the death of a close friend, who had planned a trip around the world, only to die just before departing. Badly shaken by that, Dad took out a loan to travel as soon as possible. As my husband Don would say, "Dad didn't want to die with a boat sitting in the driveway." The Dardiris had spoken so glowingly of Egypt that Mom and Dad were very excited about the trip. When they arrived, the Dardiris' family members and friends gave them the royal treatment, and Dad never regretted taking out that loan.

The trip also included stops in Portugal, Spain, and Italy, where Mom and Dad visited former students and friends. In Rome, they heard Pope Paul VI speak, and Mom told me later that she had felt he was speaking directly to her. I'm so sorry I have no letters from that period.

Around that time, Dad bought a small travel trailer, so he and Mom could travel every year to various state and national parks in New England. Not far from West Epping, New Hampshire, where Mom grew up, there was one of her favorite spots, Pawtuckaway Lake. A family friend of hers, Mrs. Blair, owned a cabin up there, so that was often Mom and Dad's destination. I vaguely remember going there when I was 3 or 4. Mom and Dad spent many enjoyable hours fishing and birdwatching at the lake, as well as shopping for antiques on their way there.

They also loved to visit Deerfield, New Hampshire, where they would time their visits to see the horses, ponies, and foals at the county fair. Mom, in particular, loved horses. Their travels also took them around the country to visit their children and grandchildren in California, Washington, Texas, and Maine.

Sometimes, Mom and Dad would take the trailer for a couple of nights to Fishermen's Memorial State Park, which was near the beach in Point Judith, Rhode Island, about ten miles from their home. The air there was bracing, and the trip was a change of pace for them. Mom loved birding and would add new species to her checklist. But after a certain visit, one bird in particular was never again welcome. Dad had just finished cooking a nice piece of steak on the grill, when a seagull swooped down and stole it. What a heartbreaker! I'm sure steak was a rare treat for Mom and Dad, and they probably had to resort to hot dogs and a can of beans.

Photo 117: Dad Barbecuing on a Camping Trip, ca. 1968

Returning to Art

After retiring, Dad resumed his interest in painting after a gap of twenty years, and began to take art lessons, probably the first he had ever had. Once a week, he would drive over to an art studio in Voluntown, Connecticut, where he experimented with various forms of art, working in oils, acrylics, and pastels. Soon, he built a comfortable studio in the basement of the house, complete with knotty pine paneled walls and a pot belly stove in the fireplace.

Free from job constraints, Dad was happy to put many hours into painting. One time, he told me that he might try a 24" by 36" oil portrait of my daughter Chris, in a standing position. In a letter to me, he wrote:

> *I have an enlargement of the print I took, and it is the most satisfactory picture I've taken of any of the grandchildren. The lighting is natural, and the shadows are just fine. The pose is, of course, natural and very relaxed and good. I shall do a study first. It is an ambitious job for me. I'm kicking myself for not taking a few portrait pictures of [your son] Jeff. He is very photogenic.*

Photo 118: Dad Painting in His Studio, ca. 1970

In January 1976, Dad resigned his position as head of the Kingston Water Department. Although it paid him about $16,000 per year, it approached a full-time job, which he did not want. Dad preferred to work part-time, running the department his own way, with freedom of time and movement. He told me back then that he and Mom would have to tighten their belts a bit, but the time had come to get out. Then he went on to say:

> *Now I will be able to put in more time painting. I hope to get back to work on Chris soon. Sold a nude yesterday [and] have some adjustments to make on a portrait commission. Also, another portrait which I may sell.*

How sweet that must have been for him to sell his first paintings. I wish he had kept records of his sales.

New Endeavors

Photo 119: Dad Painting in His Studio, ca. 1971

However, he had some health issues: frequent angina attacks and a slow heartbeat, which required him to have a pacemaker implanted in his chest. Also, when he attempted to attach a rope to his steam engine bell, which was near the edge of the roof, Dad, who was usually very careful, fell onto the patio and broke his hip. For some reason, he had been standing on a garbage can instead of a ladder. Oh my, what a mistake! Unfortunately, the hip repair was delayed a day because the hospital was being inspected for accreditation. I don't think his hip ever healed properly, since he later wrote to me that he was having increasing trouble with it.

At one time or another, Dad attempted to paint portraits of all of his grandchildren. Since none of them lived close to him, he had to rely on photos. I think he completed Christine's first. About the others, he wrote to me:

> *Teresa may be somewhat vexed with me for not having done one of her kids—possibly Pat. The fact is, I've tried without success—Pat, Nancy, and David. So, I've made the effort.*

Eventually, he completed portraits of four of his granddaughters: Christine, Patricia, Camille, and Nancy.

Photo 120: Pastel of Jesse Leon Witkoe and Nancy Lyn Hathaway, ca. 1982

Photo 121: Oil Painting of Christine Shepard Hall, 1976

Photo 122: Oil Painting of Camille Higgins, 1981

Photo 123: Watercolor of Patricia Ann Hathaway, 1977

In later years, Dad studied under Herman Itchkawich in Providence and became proficient in painting portraits and nudes, for which he won several awards. He also helped to establish a pottery studio in what was once the old Kingston Post Office. Knowing that the miniscule post office was doomed, he thought it would make a fine studio, so he wrote letters to senators and congressmen in Washington, suggesting that a new location be found for the post office. Today, the studio stands next-door to the Helme House, which is the home of the South County Art Association.[52] I'm told that one of the rooms in the studio is named for Dad.

As one can see in Dad's paintings, he worked with several models, doing much of his work from photos that he took of his subjects. The management of the figure drawing class that he was taking must have rotated among its members, because in a letter to me he said that he was

---

[52]Arlene A. Fleming, "Tom Higgins Cited for Contribution to Arts," *Providence Journal-Bulletin*, August 17, 1989, p. Z-06.

New Endeavors

in charge again. Apparently, that required him to hire a model for the class. In the same letter, he wrote:

> *I hired a professional model in her 50's, a grandma at that. She is superb. Droopy, flat-chested, but muscle tone tops, and very graceful. Our young Rhode Island School of Design graduate told me, she's tops! So, Nan, just remember as you grow older: You can be tops.*

That sure gave me a chuckle when I first read it, and it still does today!

Photo 124: The Pottery Studio in the Old Kingston Post Office Building, 2010

Dad seems to have had two favorite models, whom he painted more than once. Janice Thibedault was one. He painted her at least three times. Larry and I both have portraits of her, and I believe my nephew Robert has a full-length portrait of her as well.

The other favorite model was Becky. In a letter to me, Dad wrote:

> *I think that you may remember the slide of the painting that I did of Becky Rafanello. I put the painting in the present South County Art Association show. I have been told that folks are voting in the popular vote that it is the best painting in the show.*

This is sweet to hear, but I don't believe that it is all that good. Becky was down to see the show yesterday. She is a beauty— an eye stopper. It was apparent by the way people looked at her when we took her to lunch yesterday. We took her to the Pump House in Peace Dale, now under new management. People sure looked and I think appreciated her looks, even though it was down in Peace Dale's "left hind foot." Rachel thought that Becky was inappropriately dressed. I didn't think so, but thought that the atmosphere of the Dunes Club, the Newport Bailey's Beach Club, Alpine Club of Providence, and others more suitable. She was wearing a one-strap shoulder, one-piece bathing suit with beautiful slacks to match, with high-heeled pumps; a very expensive ensemble, not at all flashy, but quietly elegant. Becky's face and figure took care of the matter. I felt a little like Henry 'iggins in My Fair Lady. It was entertaining.

Photo 125: Painting of Becky Rafanello

New Endeavors

Photo 126: Photograph of Becky Rafanello

Photo 127: Dad Admiring His Painting of Janice Thibedault

Photo 128: Dad at a Private Showing of His Paintings

I imagine that Mom felt a little uncomfortable with all of Dad's models. It would have been hard not to be, when he described how beautiful they were with their well-formed musculature. Mom once said to me about Dad's painting "The Vintage," which always hung in a place of prominence at home, that she was always a bit jealous of "that woman."

I think I should say a word about Dad's offhand "left hind foot" remark about Peace Dale. He was being a bit of a snob there. The former Pump House Restaurant was located in an old granite building next to a small pond just outside the center of town. It's a lovely spot, but Kingston is a college town, and Peace Dale, about a mile south, is a mill town. Its small commercial area surrounds a rotary at the intersection of Kingstown Road and High Street. I remember it having a rather down-at-the-heels look, which included a liquor store and an Italian restaurant named Giro's, which catered to the college student crowd. Our family never frequented that restaurant, which is still there, along with the liquor store, while smaller businesses have come and gone.

Just beyond the rotary, there was a theater of sorts, the Peace Dale Theater, which some people called Fagan's Opera House, where all manner of entertainment was held, but probably never an opera. All of our high school basketball games were played there. But just the fact that Peace Dale had a liquor store and a restaurant with a bar colored its reputation, particularly in the 1930s through the 1950s, when we were growing up.

The town has a rich history with several historic granite buildings, including the Peace Dale Mill, the Congregational Church, the Neighborhood Guild, and the Hazard Memorial Library, all built by the Hazard family in the mid-1800s to the early 1900s. The mill had a thriving textile business at one time, and I loved to see the machines and giant rolls of colorful fabric through the massive windows that fronted one side of the building.

Growing Older

The following is excerpted from a newspaper article in 1983:

> *Tom's media are oils, pastels, watercolors, and acrylics. But his skill in them does not shut him off from new ideas—nor does his age. There were a couple of small sculpted figures in his studio at the Higgins home in Kingston, and he spoke enthusiastically of how "pottery is taking off" at the South County Art Association, with which he has long been active. Tom paints regularly. "When I have a commission, I go right to work. I don't wait for inspiration."*[53]

Rachel's Pursuits

Mom was fulfilling her creative outlets as well. She had always loved poetry, and I remember her reading poems of Robert Louis Stevenson to Teresa and me as children. Another favorite of ours was "Pirate Don Durk of Dowdee" by Mildred Meigs. When Mom was 70, she started writing poetry and even enrolled in poetry classes at the

---

[53]Bob McCreanor, "Growing Older: Finding Fulfillment in Art," *Providence Sunday Journal*, June 19, 1983, p. C-4.

university, where her professor encouraged her. She spent many hours penning verses. In 1978, Dad wrote to me about that:

> She still gets rejection slips on her poetry. It's a secret sympathy stab for me every time. But Robert Frost didn't get published until 90 years old, and Emily Dickenson never in her life! Now she is famous.

In 1982, Mom published a collection of her poetry entitled *Autumn Crocus*, which I revised in 2005 by adding some photos and family history. In an article that featured both Tom's and Rachel's artistic talents, Rachel is quoted as saying:

> Sometimes I think I should have started earlier. I write about people. Some confessional, my inner feelings, some religious. And nature—animals, flowers. But if I had started earlier, maybe I wouldn't have had anything to say.[54]

Most of Mom's poetry is fairly serious, but there is one she wrote in 1958 that just tickles my funny bone. I don't think it was ever published. Perhaps I need to add for the current generation that, in the early 1900s and even during my childhood, wearing a red petticoat or red shoes was considered a sign of poor moral character.

Red Petticoat

Oh, every day I go my way.
With downcast eye and lowered head
And no one in this town can guess
I wear a petticoat of red.
And all the neighbors say of me
Oh, what a proper girl is she
So quiet and well bred.
While morn till noon
I hum a little tune
That's running through my head
A happy, naughty, joyous tune
About my petticoat of red.

---

[54]McCreanor, "Growing Older: Finding Fulfillment in Art," p. C-4.

New Endeavors

Photo 129: Dad and Mom in San Francisco, 1984

*Photo 130: Mom (on the left) with Shirley Chisholm,
Former Congresswoman from New York (on the right)*

Although I am essentially writing here about my father, I feel I would be remiss if I didn't mention some of my mother's activities and accomplishments. She long identified herself with the peace movement and was among those who protested the Vietnam War when President Johnson spoke at the University of Rhode Island Commencement. She was a member of the Women for a Non-Nuclear Future.[55]

Photo 131: Dad and Mom (on the left) with Fellow Peace Activists Almena and Ted Neff

Mom loved meeting people of all cultures and enjoyed entertaining. She was open-minded, understanding, and honest to the core. She was also always quick with a witty response, since she loved words. Mom had a serious side to her, but in everyday comings and goings she was always pleasant, always happy, and always gracious.

Psychology, especially the Myers-Briggs Personality Tests, were especially interesting to Mom. She loved psychoanalyzing people and

---

[55]McCreanor, "Growing Older: Finding Fulfillment in Art," p. C-4.

situations, always wanting to know the whys and wherefores of people's actions. I remember once asking my dad, when he was in his 80s, if Mom's constant psychoanalyzing ever drove him nuts. He roared with laughter, but didn't really give me an answer. That was stunning to me because I'm not sure I ever made him laugh before then or after. He did laugh sometimes, but usually very quietly—so quietly that you wouldn't know he was laughing if you weren't looking at him. I'd often see him chuckling to himself when he was reading a magazine. His lips would purse together, his nose would get red, and he seemed to be trying very hard not to laugh out loud. But he would never say what had amused him.

Photo 132: Teresa and Mom, Age 95, 2001

Running Out of Steam

When Dad was in his 80s, his energy started to wane. As he wrote to me in a letter on June 22, 1982:

> *Here at home, I always have plenty to do, but somehow run out of steam—just don't have the drive, and I get out of puff. We had Tuckahoe Farms, Inc. take over our lawn care, and it looks great. The brook, after so much rain, is flowing, and I can again pump from the well. It has been powder dry for over two years. We pumped out of it for over 20 years and never thought about it. I feel awfully restless [and] want to see everyone. My cousin Lynn's death (2 mos. younger than me)—a stroke. Cousin Phil, 1980, and cousin Zed in 1979. All cousins gone.*

Dad was quite the correspondent, keeping in touch with many family members—an admirable trait. My brother, sister, and I rarely met any of his relatives, so it felt as if we really didn't have any relatives. Mom only had an unmarried brother, George, whom we rarely saw.

When Teresa or I would visit, Dad would invariably take us to meet a new acquaintance of his in town. It might be the new librarian or the woman at the bank who handled his affairs, but it was always a woman. Looking back, we now wonder if his looming Alzheimer's was a factor in this—although I suppose it's not uncommon for parents to want to show off their family.

Dad and Mom both had some major health issues in their later years. In her late 70s or early 80s, Mom needed triple bypass heart surgery. Fortunately, she came through it very well for someone her age and then attended a cardio rehab exercise program at the hospital for the next ten years.

In 1985, at the age of 83, Dad was diagnosed with retinal damage and saw his ophthalmologist every week. The doctor was optimistic, but it turned out that Dad had macular degeneration, which seriously compromised his vision. Of course, that was a terrible blow for an artist, but he continued to paint with difficulty.

On April 23, 1985, Mom wrote to me about Dad's health issues:

> *I suppose assertive women are a threat to men who feel insecure if not in complete control. I feel sorry for Dad, for I've had to take over so many things, and there's not much for him to do. It's very sad to see him sitting on the couch most of the time and sleeping, sleeping, sleeping.*

In addition to Dad's eye problems, which depressed him, this behavior could have reflected the beginning stages of his Alzheimer's disease. To get him off the couch, Mom encouraged Dad to look up information about her grandfather, who had fought in the Civil War. Mom's strategy was successful, because Dad wrote me a long letter on April 24, 1985, with detailed information about my great-grandfather:

> *George Norris Shepard, at the time of the Civil War was in the New Hampshire State Legislature. Upon President Lincoln's request for volunteers, he resigned and helped raise the 11th New Hampshire volunteers. He was given a first Lt.'s commission and later promoted to Captain. He was in command of the regiment for several months as all out-ranking officers had either been killed or wounded. He was also wounded in the hip but remained in command until a day and a half later. He had led a bayonet charge against a Confederate battery supported by riflemen when it happened. He got it in the hip, but they silenced the battery and took the riflemen prisoners. He was with the army in Virginia when General Lee surrendered, and was mustered out very soon after, on June 4, 1865.*

Dad was a genealogy buff and researched many of his ancestors and those of Mom's family, thoroughly enjoying the stories he found. He had a trove of 200 Civil War letters written by Capt. George N. Shepard, Mom's grandfather, and sometimes recounted stories from them. Many of them were quite descriptive. Some were written to his wife, Rowena, and some to his children.

He never wrote of military plans, other than to say that his company had marching orders, and he often wrote about the countryside and sent seeds, plants, or leaves home to his children. On September 28, 1862, from Camp Chase in Alexandria County (now Arlington County), Virginia, he wrote a particularly poignant letter to his wife, describing his location:

> *We are surrounded by camps on every side and by forts of some of the principal eminences. The face of the country is undulating, and over the gently swelling hilltops and down*

> *the ravines or broader valleys, the numerous campfires and illuminated tents present in the night turn a most brilliant and interesting view. It's not unlike some vast city, the form and size of tents not being distinguishable from houses by night, the animated hum of voices, the varied sounds of music. Rattling of late-returning army wagons and numerous other sounds all combine to fill the ear with sounds which the imagination easily persuades us come from such a city, and the evidence of the sense of vision not undeceiving us, the illusion is almost perfect. At a certain bugle or drum signal, all lights are extinguished about 9½ o'clock, and in the morning the truth-telling Sunlight exposes the meanness of our streets and the frailty of our edifices.*

In another letter, dated Sunday, October 26, 1862, Pleasant Valley, Maryland, my great-grandfather wrote about the appearance of Gen. Burnside riding through camp:

> *Toward night, Gen. Burnside rode through our camp at a slow pace, and the men turning out voluntarily as the news of his approach spread rapidly from tent to tent, welcomed him with boisterous shouts, in return for which, he gave them his customary salutation by lifting from his bald head the old black hat with drooping rim and holding it extended for a while in his hand, thereby enabling us to get a good view of his countenance, which was both sheltered and shaded by the ample breadth of his hat rim. I liked the looks of him, and from the first time of seeing him, have felt a strong desire to be under his command as our general. His beard and what he has of hair are black, his eyes appear to be of the same color and are shaded by heavy brows, and he is of medium height and stout frame. His countenance expresses resolute purpose and penetration, and at the same time he presents a very good-natured and comfortable appearance.*

The Rathbone (or sometimes Rathborne or Rathbun) side of Dad's family traces back to Richard Rathbone, who was born around 1574. His grandson, John Rathbun, was among the first settlers of Block Island, Rhode Island. The Higgins family is believed to be descended from Richard Higgins, a Pilgrim who emigrated to this country in the seventeenth century. In 1634, he married a woman named Lydia

New Endeavors

Chandler and was one of the founders of Eastham, Massachusetts, the only town on Cape Cod founded by Pilgrims.

My last letter from Dad arrived in 1985, since I fear his macular degeneration made it too difficult for him to write after that. Around that time, he attempted to reupholster a chair, but when I visited, I found it sitting disassembled in his studio in a sad state. I don't know if he could any longer remember how to do the work or couldn't see well enough to do it. It was distressing to see his decline.

Mom and Dad still enjoyed visiting people until about 1990, but Alzheimer's was taking its toll. Dad wasn't officially diagnosed until 1992, but the onset of the disease was probably in 1989 or earlier. We don't know why Mom fell, but trying to help Dad in some way ended up fracturing her wrist. When she was hospitalized, her doctor suggested that Dad needed supervised care in a nursing home. By this point, he had become quite difficult, particularly in the middle of the night, when he might call Mom's name repeatedly.

Mom and I moved him into the South County Nursing Center in North Kingstown, Rhode Island, where he stayed until his death, a few months later, at the age of 90. Pneumonia caused his death, which was a blessing, since it cut short what could have become a long struggle. The last time I saw Dad, he was so heavily sedated that I couldn't wake him to say goodbye. That was a heart-wrenching experience for me.

I have a couple of vivid memories of Dad when I was about five. One is of him stepping out of the bedroom, holding his trumpet. I don't know why that image is so vivid for me. I think he had been practicing. It's odd that I have no other images of him holding or playing that trumpet. Maybe we never went to his music programs.

In the other image of him from my childhood, he is all dressed up in cream-colored wool flannel trousers. I suppose I had never seen him dressed that way, but he looked very dapper. I don't know the occasion, but it must have been in the late 1930s. As always, his shoes were buffed to the hilt. Shining his shoes was almost a daily routine of his, and one that I adhered to when I wore penny loafers in the 1950s. Dad always appeared trim and fit, and quite distinguished looking. I don't remember him with anything but white hair, never bald but thinning. My brother, sister, and I are blessed with his white hair.

After Dad died, Mom continued to be active, living alone until the age of 99, just shy of her hundredth birthday. She had many dear friends who kept in touch with her and shared special days with her. The local minister was a regular visitor, and she loved to joust with him about religious philosophy. A favorite friend of hers, Carolyn Shilling, visited several times a week. Mom's daily health aides were a comfort, especially Karen Hartung and Chris Schuh.

Mom loved nothing better than birthday celebrations, when she might be invited out for several lunches. And token gifts were treasures for her—perhaps a little notebook, a pad of paper, or a new hankie. It was the thought that counted for her, not the expense of the gift. And that included gifts that she gave to others, as well as those she received. I remember getting two-dollar birthday checks for at least twenty years, which amused me every time.

I had a wonderful visit with Mom just a month before she died. Her mind was still alert as we planned her hundredth birthday party. I'm sure she was with us in spirit when we celebrated her birthday with friends and family two months later, on April 14, 2006.

What a lot of hidden memories I've dredged up with the writing of this tale. As I mentioned at the start, my purpose was to have a place to showcase Dad's art. Many of the paintings at the end of this book are taken from a collection of slides that Dad kept of his models. Others are from family collections. Without this book, it would all be scattered to the winds. As Teresa wrote to me in a letter:

> *His talent was massive. I've been thinking about his enjoyment of music, his creativity with so many forms of art, his gardening, landscaping, and his woodworking skills. He had an ability to visualize a project and follow through. It's amazing how many skills there were in which he became proficient during his lifetime.*

I totally agree with her sentiment. I admire both of my parents for many reasons: Dad for his intelligence, work ethic, many talents with his hands, and creative bent; Mom for her open-mindedness, patience, strong ethical and moral sense, and, most of all, quick wit.

In Dad's papers, I recently came across an article about him by a young man in his twenties named David Batroukha, who interviewed Dad when he was in his middle-to-late 80s. The article is entitled "Ageless," and may have been included in some type of community newsletter. At one point, David asked Dad if, given the chance to live his life over, would he be happy growing up in the era in which he was raised, or would he prefer to grow up in a different day and age.

> *He commented that he would much rather be part of today's generation. "There will be much more social change in today's world. I would like to see where those social changes will take us." He pontificated further on the future by saying women's movements such as the ERA will gain much more support, and women will be in the forefront of our growing society....*
>
> *As the two of us sat in Tom's living room and rambled on about everything from women's rights to nuclear power, I found a sublime aura enveloping us both. His easygoing, eloquent line of thought found me at the edge of my seat. All my energy concentrated on his ruddy features and his firm grasp on life. Tom's robust store of knowledge kept me in awe as the words of wisdom tumbled out of his mouth.... Tom Higgins stood out to me like an oasis in a desert. In this day and age, where red tape, government bureaucracy, and the spiraling inflation rates have everybody down, it's an enchanting experience to find a haven as I did, communicating with a man who is an oasis in life.*[56]

David's article surfaced just as I was writing this last chapter. It brought tears to my eyes as I pictured Dad talking with him, sharing his thoughts and concerns. Dad was special. He worked hard and taught us to do things right and responsibly. He was a perfectionist and passed that on to his children. He was a strong advocate of education. He taught us to love art and music. He was charming and well-liked by many. He was a family man and would have liked us all to live closer to him. But I have my cherished memories and all his letters. They will suffice.

---

[56]David Batroukha, "Ageless," *South County Community Action Newsletter*, 1981.

Photo 133: Oil Painting of Janice Thibedault

Photo 134: Portrait

Photo 135: Still Life

New Endeavors

Photo 136: Still Life, 1989

Photo 137: Still Life, 1967

Photo 138: Still Life

Photo 139: Still Life

Photo 140: Portrait

Photo 141: Landscape

Photo 142: Landscape

Photo 143: Still Life

New Endeavors

Photo 144: Still Life

Photo 145: Portrait

Photo 146: Portrait, 1975

Photo 147: Landscape

Photo 148: Landscape

Photo 149: Nude

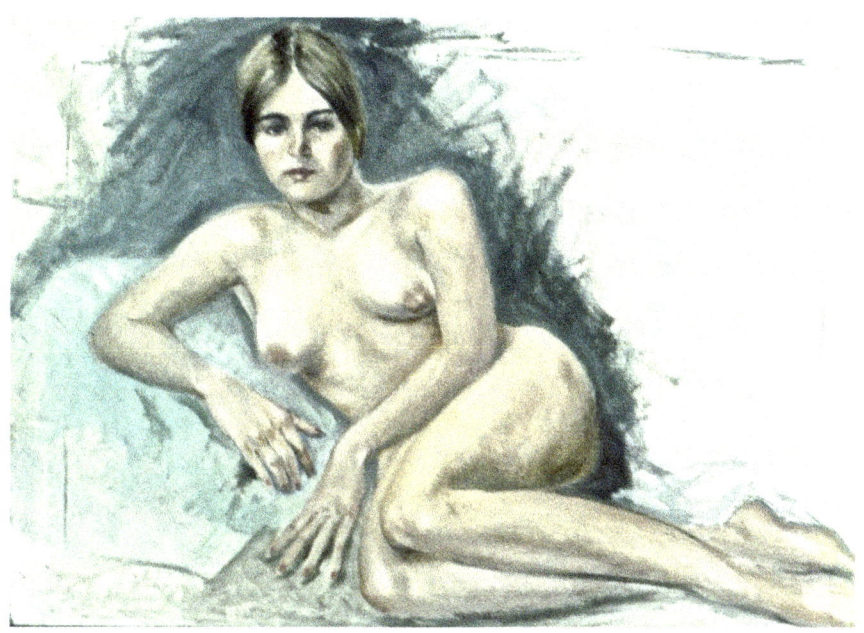

Photo 150: Nude

Photo 151: Portrait

New Endeavors

Photo 152: Portrait

Photo 153: Portrait

Photo 154: Portrait

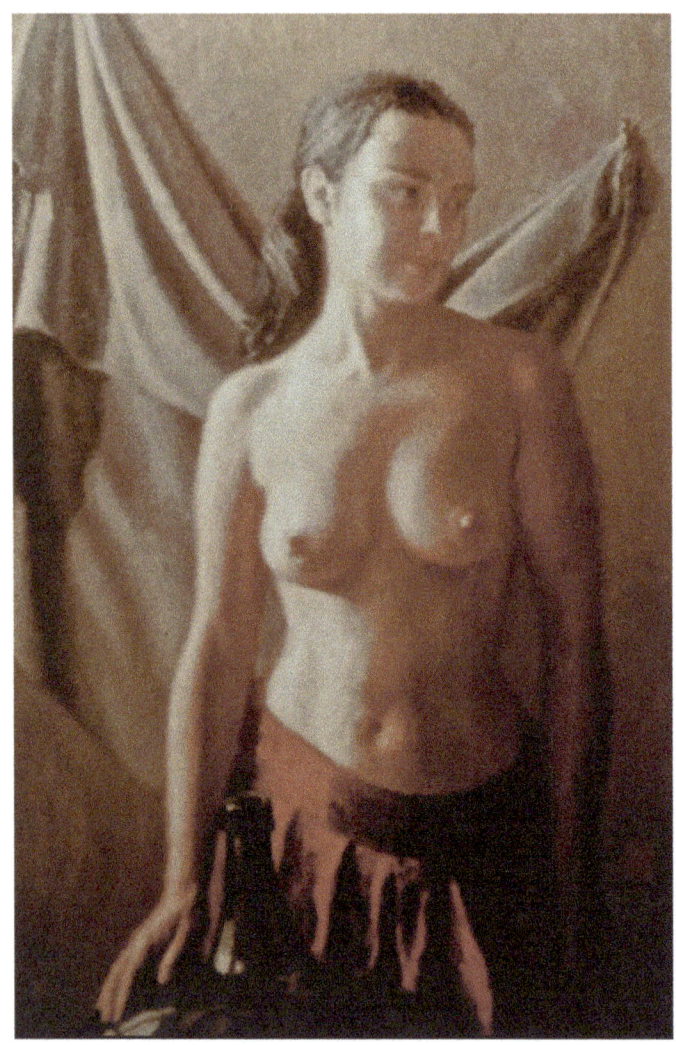

Photo 155: Nude

Photo 156: Portrait of Janice Thibedault

Photo 157: Nude

Photo 158: Nude

Photo 159: Nude

Photo 160: Nude

Photo 161: Portrait

Photo 162: Portrait, 1966

Photo 163: Nude

New Endeavors

Photo 164: Nude

Photo 165: Portrait

Photo 166: Portrait

Photo 167: Portrait

Photo 168: Becky Rafanello

Photo 169: Nude

New Endeavors

Photo 170: Nude

Photo 171: Portrait

New Endeavors

Photo 172: Portrait

Photo 173: Portrait

New Endeavors

Photo 174: Portrait

Photo 175: Portrait of Patricia Ann Hathaway, 1977

Photo 176: Portrait of Cindy, 1977

Photo 177: Nude

Photo 178: Nude

Photo 179: Nude

Photo 180: Nude

Photo 181: Portrait of Rose Etta Shepard, 1980

New Endeavors

Photo 182: Portrait

Photo 183: Landscape

Photo 184: Landscape

Photo 185: Portrait

Early Years

Photo 186: Portrait of Janice Thibedault

Thomas C. Higgins: A Man Reinvented

Photo 187: Portrait of Thomas C. Higgins, ca. 1972, by Herman Itchkawich

No Magic in Moondust

*It's not the thought of my mortality
but yours
that tarnishes the silver mornings
of my winter.
The complex threads
of my imaginings
wind and unwind.
I dream and wake
caught in a spiderweb of fear—
I cannot find you.
The sun is a gallant deceiver
for with his magic
he paints a golden world
and whispers in my ear
that you will never leave me.
But I have lived the loss of you
under the clear, cold light
of countless waning moons
and know he lies.
There is no magic in moondust.*

Rachel Shepard Higgins (1906–2006)
Autumn Crocus, Anniversary Edition

Acknowledgments

I wish to thank my husband, Don, my brother, Larry, and my sister, Teresa, for their patience during my attempts to photograph my father's paintings, and also for all their contributions to this story. My sister was so helpful in verifying records from the University of New Hampshire. My brother has a marvelous memory, as does my husband. They all recount the past with ease. That certainly is not my forte. This is a richer book because of their support.

I also wish to express my thanks to Sarina Wyatt at the University of Rhode Island Library for her help in gathering materials for me, particularly photos and historical information relating to East Farm and to Dr. Wayne Durfee, Professor Emeritus, from the University of Rhode Island, whose description of the Egg-Laying Contest was invaluable.

The staff at the Stratham Historical Society in New Hampshire shared a treasure trove of records from the Pearson family, including a family diary and a memoir by Oscar Pearson.

Mylinda Woodward, an Archives Assistant at the University of New Hampshire Dimond Library, provided records that document my father's attendance.

Tim McRoberts and Susan O'Brien, from the Michigan State University Archives & Historical Collections, were able to confirm my father's attendance and provided photos as well.

Roseanne Adams, of the Eliot Historical Society, in Maine, was a great help in providing information and photos of Nine Gables Farm and Old Bull Cottage.

Erica Luke, Executive Director of the South County History Center in Kingston, Rhode Island, was able to verify my mother's membership in the Every Tuesday Club and to find documentation of Vice President

Henry Wallace's visit to East Farm.

I thank my cousin, Terry Seifarth, for helping me with genealogical information.

Esther Rojos Soto was helpful by Photoshopping my damaged photos.

To my original content editor, Janine deBoisblanc, who unfailingly gave me support, encouragement, and spot-on suggestions for improvement, I owe my deepest gratitude.

And most especially my thanks go to Paul Weisser, Ph.D., my final editor, with whom I spent many hours. He was exceptional, always on target with his criticisms, engaging to work with, and very supportive. He attempted to educate me on the use of commas, but I am still a bit of a failure on that score. There would be no book without Paul's help.

There are the friends and family members who graciously read my manuscript and gave me encouragement and suggestions for improvement. These include: my husband, Don, who was always willing to read a new section; my brother, Larry, for his phenomenal memory; my sister, Teresa, for her corroboration of events; Judith Dillingham, Dale Westbrook, and Liz Conescue, who were all loyal readers; Pat Bowes, who listened to my endless prattle about the book; my son, Jeff, and his wife, Leslie, for help with headings; my daughter, Christine, for her photos of East Farm; a special nod to Noel Thomas, Sr., for the inspiration for my title; and a special thanks to Susan Dannenfelser for her immense help and artistic talent in arranging the collection of the paintings at the end of this book. Thank you all.

Finally, I must acknowledge the fact that my father saved many letters that were invaluable for my research. Thank you, Dad, for saving all those letters. And thank you, Mom, for your journals and inspiring poetry.

Index

A&P Food Markets, 114
'Abdu'l-Bahá (Bahá'í prophet), 44
Adams, Roseanne, 223
Adamsville (Rhode Island), 127
African Americans, 99, 100
"Ageless" (article about Dad), 165
Agricultural Extension Service, 106, 113, 116
Air Raid Warden (Dad), 85
Alexander, Dr. Nicholas (Ph.D.), 83
Alpha Tau Alpha fraternity, 22
Alpine Club (Providence, Rhode Island), 152
Alzheimer's disease (Dad's), 160, 161, 163
American Christian Ashram, 85
Andover Theological Seminary, 25, 35
Animal Pathology Department (East Farm), 95
Anti-nuclear activities (Mom's), 85
Art Studio (Dad's), 94, 145–147, 150, 151, 155, 163
Atlee, Elsie Higgins, 4
Atlee, Zed (Dad's cousin), 4, 8, 26, 30, 105, 160
Autumn Crocus, Anniversary Edition, xiii, xv, 156, 221
Avian coccidiosis (parasitic disease), 113

Bachelor's degree (Dad's), 105
Bahá'í religion, 44–46
Bahá'u'lláh, founder of the Bahá'í religion, 44, 45
Bailey's Beach Club (Newport, Rhode Island), 152
Balloonist, 55
Bantam chickens, 102
Barbecues, 108, 117, 136–138, 145
Barn fire, 76, 77

Barns, 9, 32, 55, 57, 98, 101
Barred Rock chickens, 49
Baseball, 92, 93, 100
Bates, Dr. Reuben, M.D., 107, 138
Batik, 69, 70
Batroukha, David, 165
Bausch & Lomb Science Award, 122
Beck, Rev, John D., 128
Bedell, Stewart (Don's uncle), 134
Bedspread, 131, 132
Beta Phi Corporation, 138
Bicycles, 12, 35, 85, 93, 102, 117
Big Pine, California, 134
Birthdays, 11, 76, 82, 164
Biscuit City (neighborhood of Kingston, Rhode Island), 141–143
Black Diamond, Washington, 26, 28, 81
Blair, Mary Folsom, 144
Block Island, Rhode Island, 162
Board of Wardens, 141
Boston, Massachusetts, 46, 123
Bowes, Pat, 224
Boxing, 118
Braided rugs, 131
Bressler, Dr. Raymond George (Ph.D.), 74, 105
Brightman, M. H., 49, 50, 52
Brookline, Massachusetts, 38
Browning, Dean Harold W. ("Bulldog"), 134
Buick (Dad's), 107
Bunker, 76
Burnside, General Ambrose, 162
Butte, Montana, 26, 28

Calhoun, Isaac P., 28
California, 86, 134, 135, 144
Cameras, 81, 85
Camp Chase (Alexandria County [now Arlington County], Virginia), 161, 162

Canada, 3, 44, 46
Cancer, 73, 124
Candling eggs, 95, 115
Cape Cod, 101, 163
Card parties, 21, 23
Cass County, Michigan, 3
Cassopolis Community Band, 41
Cassopolis, Michigan, 40, 41
Cat boats, 93
Chandler, Lydia, 163
Chanticleer (rooster), 102
Checkers (the game), 92
Chemistry sets, 82, 83
Cheney, Washington, 135
Chi (life energy), 124
Chicken brooders. 49
Chicken coops, 66, 77, 99, 102
Chicken of Tomorrow contest, 114
Chickens, 9, 23, 31, 36, 42, 49, 59, 60, 66, 77, 89, 90, 99, 100, 102, 103, 107, 112, 114–117, 126, 127, 137, 138
Chief Dowagiac (see Dowagiac, Chief), 4
China, 36
Ching Foh Bau, 36, 37, 44
Chisholm, Shirley, 157
Christmas, 44, 65, 91, 102, 111
Church activities (Mom's), 82, 88
Cider, 96, 97
Cindy (model), 209
Civilian Conservation Corps, 85
Civil War (U.S.), 161, 162
Clambakes, 117
Classical music, 108
Clothing label, 121
Coccidiosis (parasitic disease), 113
Colorado, 86
Conescue, Liz, 224
Connecticut, 137, 145

Cooperative Extension Education Service, 89
Cotton Manufactory (cotton mill), 142
Countway Library of Medicine, Harvard University, 126
Cram, Judith H., xvii
Crawford, T. Stephen, Dean of Engineering, 111, 118
Creelman, Margaret Jane, xvii

Dannenfelser, Susan, 224
Dardiri, Dr. Ahmed H. (DVM), 144
Dardiri, Lucille, 144
Darwin, Charles, 81
Daycare centers, 88
deBoisblanc, Janine, 224
Deerfield, New Hampshire, 144
Delaplane, Dr. John Paul (DVM), 78, 96, 113–115, 119
Demonstration Vegetable Garden, 89
Depression era, 54
Detention Camps (Japanese), 86
Detroit, Michigan, 1, 3
Dickens, Charles, 81
Dickenson, Emily, 156
Dillingham, Judith, 224
Dimond Library (University of New Hampshire), 223
Dogs, 15, 46, 54
Dover, New Hampshire, 39
Dowagiac, Chief, 4
Dowagiac Drill Company, 5
Dowagiac High School, 10, 11
Dowagiac High School Band, 10–12
Dowagiac, Michigan, 1, 4, 5, 8, 10, 11
Dowsing (see Water dowsing)
Driving lessons, 81, 82
Dunes Club (Narragansett, Rhode Island), 152
Dungarees, 99
Durant, Henry, 123
Durfee, Dr. Wayne K. (Ph.D.), 58, 59, 223
Durgin, Elizabeth, xvii

Durham, New Hampshire, 19, 22, 23
Dutch door, 82
Dynamite, 76

Easter, 111
Eastern States Exposition, 116, 141
East Farm, 57–61, 76–79, 82, 90, 95–99, 105, 107, 117, 121, 123, 127–129, 137, 224
East Farm Poultry staff, 78, 96
Eastham, Massachusetts, 163
Edwards Hall (Rhode Island State College), 109
Edwards, Ivy, 46
Egg-laying contests, 57–59, 107, 123, 223
Eggs, 49, 54, 57–60, 73, 95, 96, 99, 102, 103, 107, 114–116, 123, 127, 141, 223
Egypt, 144
Eisenhower, Gen. Dwight D., xvi
Eisenhower-style jackets, xvi, 112
11th New Hampshire Volunteers, 161
Eliot Historical Society (Maine), 223
Eliot, Maine, 43, 46
Elk Point, South Dakota, 28
Endo, Harry, 86
Endo, Mary, 86–88, 113
Equal Rights Amendment (ERA), 165
Erector sets, 82
Every Tuesday Club (women's literary group), 63, 64, 223
Exeter, New Hampshire, 19, 20, 23
Experiment Station (see Agricultural Extension Service), 38, 58, 114
Explosives, 76
Extension poultryman, 105, 106
Extrasensory perception (ESP), 124

Fagan's Opera House (see Peace Dale Theater)
Family genealogical information, xvi
Father James Greenan, 88
Federal Land Bank loans, 54

Fellowship of Reconciliation Program, 85
Fiestaware dishes, 46
Fight between Tom and Max, 42, 43
Figure drawing class (Dad's), 150
Fire, 76, 77
Fisherman's Memorial State Park (Rhode Island), 144
Flint-Adaskin furniture store, 52
Folsom family, 25
Food and Drug Administration, 125, 126
Football, 92
4-H egg and poultry judging teams, 141
4-H Poultry and Egg Marketing (pamphlet by Dad), 116, 117
Fowl cholera (bacterial disease), 113
Frazier, Birdie, 5–7
Free-range chickens, 60, 99
Fremont, New Hampshire, 22
Frost, Robert, 156
Fruit, 74, 91, 96, 97, 117
Fruit growers' meeting, 117
Fry, Dr. Marion (Ph.D.), 131
Future Farmers of America, 116, 141

Games, 21, 92
Gandhi, Mahatma, 85
Gas allotment, 112
Germany, 133
Gettysburg, 119
Gilbert and Sullivan, 109
Gilbert, Dr. Basil E. (Ph.D.), 9, 58
Gildow, Dr. Elton M. (DVM), 39
Gildow, Florence, 39
Gill, Massachusetts, xvi, 110, 111
Giro's Restaurant, 154
Glick, Sarah, xix
Golf, 92
Gough farm, 58, 60
Graduation (Dad's), 11, 37, 105, 106

Grand Central Art Galleries (New York), 74
Grange scholarship, 32
Grasscloth wallpaper, 129
Great Depression, 49, 54
Greenan, Father James, 88
Greene, Sarah, 93
Green Hall (Rhode Island State College), 79, 133
Gross, Helen, 128

Hall, Christine Shepard, 103, 135, 136, 145, 146, 148, 149, 224
Hall, Donald Hinckley, 19, 133–135, 138, 144, 223, 224
Hall, Jeffrey Higgins, 135, 146, 224
Hall, Leslie, 224
Hall, Nancy Higgins, ii, vii–ix, xv, xvi, 3, 5, 7, 10, 11, 13, 15, 16, 19, 21–23, 26, 28, 29, 32–35, 37, 38, 40, 42, 43, 45–47, 51–55, 60–62, 64, 66–69, 73, 76, 77, 80–83, 85, 86, 88, 89, 91–113, 115–125, 127–138, 141, 142, 144–146, 148, 150, 151, 154–156, 158–161, 163–165, 223, 224, back cover
Hannah Robinson Tower, 85
Harrisburg, Pennsylvania, 116, 141
Hart, Michigan, 14
Hartung, Karen, 164
Harvard University, 25, 35, 126
Hathaway, Arthur, 127, 128, 134, 135
Hathaway, David, 135, 148
Hathaway, Jesse Leon Witkoe, 148
Hathaway, Nancy Lyn, 39, 135, 148
Hathaway, Patricia Ann, 135, 148, 150, 208
Hathaway, Robert, 135, 151
Hathaway, Teresa Rathborne (Sister), vii, xv, xvi, 4, 9, 15, 37, 51, 52, 54, 55, 59, 64, 68, 69, 76, 77, 80–83, 88, 91–93, 95–103, 106–109, 111–113, 115, 117–124, 127, 128, 133–135, 137, 138, 148, 155, 159, 160, 164, 223, 224, back cover
Hawaii, 85
Hawaiian guitar lessons (Larry's), 109
Haynes, Leslie, xvii
Hazard family, 155

Hazard Memorial Library (Peace Dale, Rhode Island), 155
Head House, 59
Head Start, 82
Heidelberg College, 128, 133
Helme House (Kingston, Rhode Island), 150
"Henrietta" (Larry's Model A Ford), 123
Hess, Marian, 133, 135
Higbee, Violet B., 137, 138
Higgins, Camille Elizabeth, 135, 148, 149
Higgins, Caroline Rathbun, xx, 2, 4, 8, 10, 40, 42
Higgins, Claude (Tom's uncle), 4, 54, 55, 94
Higgins Drive (Kingston, Rhode Island), 141
Higgins family gathering, 4
Higgins farm (see also Rolling Meadows farm), 73
Higgins, Heather Sturgis, 135
Higgins, James Maxwell, 1, 2, 4, 7, 12, 40, 42, 43, 94
Higgins, James T., xviii
Higgins, Janeth, 3
Higgins, Jay P., 1–4, 8, 10, 15, 36, 40, 42, 54, 73, 92–94, 105, 107, 108
Higgins, Laurel Shepard, 135
Higgins, Lawrence Shepard (Brother), xv, xvi, 11, 35, 54, 55, 63, 64, 66–69, 72, 75, 76, 80, 82–85, 88, 92, 93, 98, 100–106, 108–112, 118, 119, 121–124, 129, 133–135, 137, 138, 141, 151, 160, 164, 223, 224, back cover
Higgins, Leona Gifford, 4
Higgins, Lois (Max's wife), 40, 42
Higgins, Mabel Palmer, 1–4, 10, 40, 42, 43, 55, 73, 74, 93, 105
Higgins, Margaret Ann (Max's daughter), 42
Higgins, Marian (see Marian Hess)
Higgins, Mary A., xviii
Higgins, Maxwell ("Max"), 7, 10, 12, 40, 42, 43, 94
Higgins, Nancy Palmer (see Hall, Nancy Higgins)
Higgins, Rachel Elizabeth Shepard (Mom), xiii, xv–xvii, xxii 25, 26, 29–44, 46, 47, 49, 50, 52–54, 60–69, 81, 82, 85, 86, 88, 91–93, 100, 102–108, 112, 115, 116, 118, 120, 121, 124, 128–130, 133–135, 137–139, 144–146, 152, 154–161, 163–165, 221, 223, 224, back cover

Higgins, Richard, 162, 163
Higgins, Teresa Rathborne (see Hathaway, Teresa Rathborne)
Higgins, Thomas Craven (Dad), front cover, xv–xxi, 1–15, 17–25, 34–44, 46, 47, 49–55, 57, 58, 60–62, 64–78, 80–83, 85, 88, 91–96, 98–103, 105–116, 118–121, 123–125, 127–139, 141–148, 150–165, 220, 223, 224, back cover
Higgins, Thomas Wesley, 135
Higgins, Thomas Titus, xx, 4, 8–10, 13, 14, 40, 42
High School Self-Taught (book), 76
High Street (Peace Dale, Rhode Island), 154
Hirohito, Emperor of Japan, 87
Hobbs, Frank, 22
Hodgkin's Disease, 73
Holy Trinity Monastery, Jordanville, New York, 84
Homer, 81
Hope Lodge #25 of the Masonic Order, 107
Horticultural Building, 96
Hurricanes, 103, 128, 138
Hy-Line Company, 107

Ice cream, 80, 122
Infectious bronchitis, 114
Institute for Orgonomic Science, 125
Italy, 127, 144
Itchkawich, Herman, 150, 220

Japan, 21, 85, 87, 88
Japanese-Americans, 87
Japanese relocation policies, 85, 86
Jefferson Township, Michigan, 8, 10, 11
Johnson, President Lyndon B., 158
Jordanville, New York, 83, 84
Joshua Tree National Park, 134

Kingston Congregational Church, 88, 107, 120
Kingston Hill Grammar School, 83, 100
Kingston Improvement Association, 107

Kingston Players, 61, 62
Kingston Post Office, 150, 151
Kingston, Rhode Island, 49–52, 58, 61–64, 77, 83, 85, 86, 93, 100–102, 107, 127, 128, 132–134, 141–142, 146, 150, 151, 154, 155, 223
Kingston Volunteer Fire Department, 77, 141
Kingston Water Department, 141, 146
Kingstown Road (Kingston, Rhode Island), 123, 128, 154
Kummer, Clare (playwright), 61

Lake Winnipesaukee, New Hampshire, 85
Larkin's Pond, West Kingston, Rhode Island, 93
Las Cruces, New Mexico, 135
Layer chickens, 49
League of Women Voters, 82
Lee, General Robert E., 161
Leghorn chickens, 49, 127
Library of Congress, 126
Library Science, 123
Lincoln Logs, 82
Lincoln, President Abraham, 161
Literary Digest magazine, 74, back cover
Little Compton (Rhode Island), 116, 127
Little Rest, Rhode Island, 50
Loom, four-harness (Nancy's), 131, 132
Lone Ranger, The (radio program), 108
Loring, Paule, 137
Louisiana, 138
Loveday, Lionel, 46
Luce, Governor Cyrus G., 8
Luke, Erica, 223

Macular degeneration (Dad's), 160, 161, 163
Main, Billy, 85
Maine, 32, 33, 41, 43, 46, 111, 125, 126, 144, 223
Main's Jewelry Shop, 85, 108
Manse, church, 101
Maple syrup, 91

Marching band music, 108
Marriage, xv, 3, 35, 38, 39, 47, 57, 128, 133, 134, back cover
Marsalis, Wynton, 11,12
Maryland, 162
Massachusetts, xvi, 38, 46, 110, 111, 116, 123, 137, 141, 163
Master Gardener Field House, 89, 90
Master of Science degree (Dad's), 133
McKinley Grammar School, 5
McNulty, Police Chief Walter, 124
McRoberts, Tim, 223
Meigs, Mildred, 155
Mexico, 135
Mexico City, 135
Michigan, 2, 8, 13–15, 17, 19, 40, 41, 43, 52, 54, 75, 93–94, back cover
Michigan Agricultural College (M.A.C.), 13–15, 17
Michigan State Legislature, 8
Michigan State Normal School, 2
Michigan State University, 13, 75, 223
Mighty Moe ice cream truck, 122
Military encampments, 91
Minstrel shows, 21
Model A Ford, 123
Model T Fords, 12
Monastery chapel (model), 83, 84
Monopoly (the game), 92
Montana, 26, 28
Montreal, Canada, 44, 46
Moody, Dwight L., 110
Morgan, Mr., 28
Morgan, Mrs., 28
Motorcycle, Harley, 34, 35
Mt. Hermon School for Boys, xvi, 110–112, 118
Movies, 91
Mowing lawn, 102
Muir Woods National Monument, 134
Music, 108, 109, 164, 165
Myers-Briggs Personality Tests, 158

My Fair Lady, 152

Naps (Mom's), 82
Narragansett fire department, 77
Narragansett, Rhode Island, 77, 108, 152
Narragansett Times, xv, 87
National Aeronautics Society, 83
National Park Service, 135
Native Americans, 110
Naval Reserve, 85
Neff, Almena, 158
Neff, Ted, 158
Neighborhood Guild (Peace Dale, Rhode Island), 109, 155
New England, 144
New Hampshire, 15, 17, 19–25, 32, 36–39, 43, 49, 69, 75, 85, 106, 144, 161, 223, back cover
New Hampshire State College (also see University of New Hampshire), 19, 25, 32, 35, 43, 49
New Hampshire State Legislature, 161
New Hampshire, University of, Agricultural Experiment Station, 38
New Mexico, 135
Newport, Rhode Island, 152
Newton Avenue, Narragansett, Rhode Island, 108
New York, 157
New York City, 74
New York Public Library, 38
Niles High School, 11
Niles High School Orchestra, 11
Nine Gables farm, 43, 46, 223
"No Magic in Moondust" (Mom's poem), 221
"Nook, The," 92, 108
Norris, Hannah, xvii, 161
Northeastern Poultry Producers Council (egg-grading school), 116
Northfield School for Girls. 110
North Kingstown, Rhode Island, 163

Oberlin College, 128

O'Brien, Susan, 223
Ohio, 128
"Old Bull" Cottage, 44, 223
Olivet Congregational Church, 28
Orchards, 40, 58, 76, 91, 96–97
Orgone accumulators, 124–126

Pacifism (Mom's), 85, 88
Painting (Dad's), xv, 74, 94, 95, 101, 105, 107, 130, 145–147, 149–155, 160, 166, 223
Palmer, Gideon A., xvii
Palmer, Ida, 3
Palmer, John, 3
Palmer, Mabel (see Higgins, Mabel Palmer)
Palmer, Samuel Nathaniel, xxi
Paranormal phenomena, 124
Patience (Gilbert and Sullivan operetta), 109
Pawtuckaway Lake, New Hampshire, 144
Peace Dale Congregational Church, 155
Peace Dale Mill, 155
Peace Dale, Rhode Island, 109, 152, 154–155
Peace Dale Theater (or Fagan's Opera House), 155
"Pea Pod" (Don's VW), 133
Pearl Harbor, Hawaii, 85, 87, 88
Pearson, Dorothy, 19, 20, 49
Pearson, Frank, 17–19, 21, 49
Pearson, Georgiana, 19
Pearson, Grace, 19
Pearson, Margaret, 19, 20, 22, 23
Pearson, Oscar, 19, 23, 223
"Peggy" (stick and ball game), 21
Pennsylvania, 116, 141
Peterson, Arnold W. (reporter), xv
Phi Gamma Delta fraternity, 138
Philippines, 37
Philips Exeter Academy, 20
Photo enlarger (Larry's), 85

Piano, 19, 131, 133
Pigs, 9, 13, 98, back cover
Pilgrims, 162, 163
"Pirate Don Durk of Dowdee" (poem), 155
Plaster cast of Larry's head, 69, 72
Playhouse, 82, 83
Pleasant Valley, Maryland, 162
Plymouth (1937 car), 80
Plymouth Rock chickens, 49
Pneumonia (Dad's), 163
Poetry (Mom's), 155, 156
Point Judith, Rhode Island, 144
Pomeroy's Past (three-act comedy), 61
Pomology Department (East Farm), 96, 97, 117
Poole, Mary Ellen, xvii
Pope Paul VI, 144
Portugal, 144
Potawatomi Indian Tribe, 5
Potter family, 100
Potter, Perry, 100
Pottery studio, 150, 151
Poultry, 23, 35, 36, 38–40, 43, 49, 58–60, 76–79, 90, 94–96, 98, 99, 112–117, 119, 125, 127, 129, 137, 141
Poultry buildings, 23, 60, 61, 76, 77, 79, 99
Poultry Department (East Farm), 115, 117, 137
Poultry Department office building, 76, 94, 95, 118
Poultry Department staff, 78, 96
Poultry hatchery, 95
Poultrymen, 59
Providence Journal, The, 77, 137
Providence, Rhode Island, 52, 80, 123, 150, 152
Psychology (Mom's interest), 158
Pump House Restaurant, 152, 154

Queen of Romania, 46
Quonset huts, 94, 95

Rabbit hutch, 102, 103
Radios, 85, 108
Rafanello, Becky, 151–153, 201
Ralshoven, Julius (painter), 74
Rangely, Maine, 126
Ranger Hall (University of Rhode Island), 83
Rathbone, Richard, 162
Rathbun, Caroline, xx
Rathbun, John, 162
Rathbun, Lucius, xix
Rationing, 91, 101
"Red Petticoat" (Mom's poem), 156
Reich, Dr. Wilhelm, 124–126
Religion (Mom's), 85, 164
Reserve Officers' Training Corps (ROTC), 22, 86
Return of Peter Grimm, The (play), 62
Rhode Island, 49, 51, 52, 80, 81, 91, 93, 108, 114, 116, 123, 127, 141-144, 150, 152, 154–155, 162, 163, 223, back cover
Rhode Island Agricultural Experiment Station, 58
Rhode Island College of Agriculture and Mechanical Arts (see also Rhode Island State College), 49, back cover
Rhode Island Master Gardeners Association, 89
Rhode Island Red Centennial Committee, 127
Rhode Island Red chickens, 49, 116, 126, 127
Rhode Island Red pin, 127
Rhode Island School of Design, 151
Rhode Island State College (R.I.S.C.; also see University of Rhode Island), 49, 50, 58, 61, 63, 74, 77, 83, 86, 95, 105, 109, 116, 118, back cover
Rhode Island State Department of Agriculture, 49
Rhode Island State Trooper, 82
Ringling Circus, 12
Robinson family, 100
Robinson Female Seminary, 20
Robinson, Frank, 81
Robinson, Prudence ("Prudy"), 76, 78, 81
Rolling Meadows farm, Michigan, 40–42, 73

Romania, 46
Rome, Italy, 144
Roosevelt, President Franklin Delano, 85, 107
Round, Leon, 98
Route 1 (Post Road, Rhode Island), 85
Route 108 (Kingstown Road, Rhode Island), 58, 90, 99, 100
Route 138 (Mooresfield Road, Rhode Island), 85

Sailboats, 93
Salt Pond, Wakefield, Rhode Island, 93
Saluki dogs, 46
San Antonio, Texas, 135
San Bernadino, California, 135
San Francisco, California, 28, 32, 134, 135, 157
San Francisco State College, 134, 135
Savage, Nettie, 3
Savings bonds, 88
Schepp Foundation, 110
Schlenker family, 86
Schopflocher, Florence ("Kitty" or "Lorol") 43–46
Schopflocher, Siegfried, 44, 46
Schreiber, Fred, 123, 124
Schuh, Chris, 164
Seattle, Washington, 26
"Secret Weapon" (newspaper article), 87
Seifarth, Terry, 224
Self-portrait, 69
Senior project at college (Nancy's), 131, 132
Shadow, The (radio program), 108
Shakespeare, William, 81
Shepard, Captain George Norris (Mom's grandfather), xxii, 28, 161
Shepard, George, 29, 31, 43, 160
Shepard, Herman Thyng, 25–29, 32, 33, 35, 37–39, 41–43, 50, 52, 81
Shepard, Rachel (see Higgins, Rachel Shepard)
Shepard, Rose Etta Smith, 29–31, 35, 37–39, 88, 214
Shepard, Rowena Thyng, xxii, 26, 28, 29, 161
Shepard, Samuel, xii, xvii, 21

Shilling, Carolyn, 164
Shoes (Dad's), 163
Shurter, Florence Higgins, 4
Shurter, Frederick, 4
Shurter, Lynn, 4, 8, 160
Shurter, Philip ("Phil"), 4, 8, 160
Skunks, 99
Slaves, 110
Smith, Charles F., xvii
Smith, Louise, 19
Smith, Rose Etta, (see Shepard, Rose Etta)
Smith, Stanley, 76, 78
Smith, Susan Minerva, xvii
Snow and ice, 18, 20, 21, 72, 80, 96, 122
So's Your Old Antique (play), 61
Soto, Esther Rojos, 224
Southbridge, Massachusetts, 111
South County Art Association, 107, 150, 151, 155
South County History Center, 63, 64, 223
South County Nursing Center, 163
South County Orchestra, 108, 109
South Dakota, 26, 28
South Kingstown fire department, 77
South Kingstown High School, 86, 88, 120, 122
South Kingstown High School Spanish Club, 88
South Kingstown Land Trust, 143
Spain, 144
Spatter painting, 101
Spokane, Washington, 135
Springfield, Massachusetts, 111, 141
Steadman, May, 109
Stereopticon slide projector, 21
Stevenson, Robert Louis, 155
Stratham Historical Society, 223
Stratham, New Hampshire, 17, 23, 24
Stuart, Prof. Homer O., 78, 106, 107
Sugar rationing, 91

Suicide doors, 80
Suits (made by Dad), xvi, 68, 110, 112, 120, 121, 152
Sulfaquinoxaline (antimicrobial agent), 113
Sump pump, 128
Sunday trips, 80
Sunny Ridge Farm, 49, 53, 54
Swimming lessons, 93

Tarantula bite, 46
Tavern Hall Club, 107
Taylor, Raymond, 76, 78, 98
Texas, 135, 144
Textiles and clothing, 131, 133
Thermite, 83
Thiebedault, Janice (model), 151, 153, 166, 189, 219
Thomas, Noel, Sr., 224
Thyng, Dudley, xvii
Tilbury, Canada, 3
Titanic, The (ship), 72
Tomatoes, 52, 88, 91
Tom's fourth-grade class, 6
Tom's retirement photo, 144
Tom's second-grade class, 5
Tom's third-grade class, 5, 6
Tornadoes, 9
Toys, 82
"Tribute, A" (Rachel's poem), xiii
Triple bypass heart surgery (Mom's), 160
Trumpets, front cover, xv, 11–13, 20, 69, 108, 109, 163
Tuckahoe Farms, Inc., 160
Tufts Medical School, 123, 134
Twins, xvi, 64, 66, 74, 77, 112, 115, 121, 124, 134, 135, back cover

United Nations family, 135
United States Department of Agriculture, 114
Universal military training, 92
University of New Hampshire (also see New Hampshire State College),

21–24, 35–39, 75, 106, 223, 224
University of New Hampshire Agricultural Experiment Station, 38
University of New Hampshire band, 19, 21–24
University of Rhode Island (see also Rhode Island State College), 58, 59, 63, 89, 111, 118, 113, 123, 127, 129, 133–135, 137, 138, 141, 144, 156, 158, 223
University of Rhode Island Library, 133, 223
University of Rhode Island Master Gardeners Association, 89, 111
Usquepaug, Rhode Island, 100, 101

Valedictorian, 122
Vegetables, 54, 91
Victory Gardens, 88–91
Vietnam War, 158
"Vintage, The" (Dad's painting), 74, 75, 154
Virginia, 161, 162
Volkswagen sedan (Don's), 133
Voluntown, Connecticut, 145

Wakefield, Rhode Island, 85, 93, 109, 120
Wales, Prof. Royal, 109
Wallace, Henry, Vice President, 107, 223, 224
Wallpaper (see Grasscloth wallpaper)
Walmsley family, 100
Warner, Bob, 85
Washing machines, 81, 117, 118
Washington County Jail House, 77
Washington, DC, 126, 150
Washington (state), 26, 81, 135, 144
Watercolors, 72
Water dowsing, 124, 125, 128
Weaving, 131, 132
Weisser, Paul, Ph.D. (editor), 224
Weldin, Dr. John (Ph.D.), 74, 76, 78, 105
Wells (water), 100
Westbrook, Dale, 224
West Epping, New Hampshire, vi–vii, 25, 26, 28, 43, 69, 144

West Kingston, 93
West Kingston Grange, 107
West Springfield, Massachusetts, 116
Whitmore, Orleta, 8–10
Wiley family, 3
Wiley, Dr. William (Ph.D.), 96
Wiley, James, xvii,
Wiley, Margaret E., xxi
Wilhelm Reich Museum, 126
Williams' farm, 55
Wilson, President Woodrow, 30
Winchester rifle, 103
Witkoe, Jesse Leon, 148
Women for a Non-Nuclear Future, 158
Women's political movements, 165
Woodcarving, 69, 73, 164
Woodchuck, 103
Woodmansee, Frank, 96, 99
Woodward, Dr. Carl (Ph.D.), 113,
Woodward, Mylinda, 223
Works Progress Administration (WPA), 76
World War I, 10, 14, 17
World War II, xvi, 37, 85–87, 91, 92, 95, 98, 108, 109, 112, 114, 138
Wyatt, Sarina, 223

York Beach, Maine, vi, 32, 33
Ypsilanti, Michigan, 2, 3

My parents moved five times in their first year of marriage. That doesn't sound like a path to success. But I see six pivotal points in Dad's life, which are fully described in this book:

The first, in 1920, relates (would you believe it?) to a black Hampshire pig in Michigan.

The second is his marriage in 1928 in New Hampshire to Rachel Shepard, my mother.

The third is their move to Rhode Island in 1929 and Dad's subsequent hiring as a farm manager at Rhode Island State College.

The fourth is the birth of their son, Lawrence, in 1932.

The fifth is the birth of their twin daughters, Nancy and Teresa, in 1935.

And finally, the sixth and perhaps most pivotal point is Dad's pastel drawing in 1936 of a woman on the cover of *Literary Digest* magazine.

These events all coalesced together in Dad's drive to successfully excel at whatever he attempted. And excel he did.

—Nancy Higgins Hall

Nancy Higgins Hall graduated with a degree in Textile & Clothing from the University of Rhode Island, foregoing that career to take a job at the University Library while her husband finished college. They moved to San Francisco where she worked at the San Francisco State College Library followed by a hiatus to raise a son and daughter. Once her son and daughter reached school age, she resumed her library career by working at the Orinda Union School District for 28 years.

ABOOKS

ALIVE Book Publishing and ALIVE Publishing Group
are imprints of Advanced Publishing LLC,
3200 A Danville Blvd., Suite 204, Alamo, California 94507

Telephone: 925.837.7303
alivebookpublishing.com

www.ingramcontent.com/pod-product-compliance
Lightning Source LLC
Chambersburg PA
CBHW050927240426
43670CB00023B/2958